The Amish Cook

The Amish Cook

Recollections and Recipes from an Old Order Amish Family

Elizabeth Coblentz with Kevin Williams

Photographs by Laurie Smith

Ten Speed Press
Berkeley / Toronto

In Memoriam
Benjamin Coblentz
(1931–2000)

Ten Speed Press
Box 7123
Berkeley, California 94707
www.tenspeed.com

Distributed in Australia by Simon & Schuster Australia, in Canada by Ten Speed
Press Canada, in New Zealand by Southern Publishers Group, in South Africa by
Real Books, in Southeast Asia by Berkeley Books, and in the United Kingdom and
Europe by Airlift Book Company.

Cover and text design by Nancy Austin
Photographs on pages 76, 113, and 147 are courtesy of Bill Coleman
(www.AmishPhoto.com). All other photographs by Laurie Smith.

Some of the material in this book was originally published in *The Amish Cook
Cookbook,* copyright © 1993 by Kevin L. Williams, Oasis Newsfeatures, Inc.

Library of Congress Cataloging-in-Publication Data
Coblentz, Elizabeth.
  Recollections and recipes from an old order Amish family / Elizabeth
Coblentz with Kevin Williams.
    p. cm.
Includes index.
  ISBN 1-58008-214-9
  1. Cookery, Amish. 2. Amish—United States—Social life and customs.
I. Williams, Kevin. II. Title.
  TX715 .C643 2002
  641.5'66—dc21
                              2002004200

Printed in China
First printing, 2002

1 2 3 4 5 6 7 8 9 10 — 06 05 04 03 02

Table of Contents

Acknowledgments

Thanks goes to my daughters Verena and Susan, who still live at home with me. Also thank you to all my children and their families, including my daughters Liz, Leah, Lovina, and Emma, and my sons, Amos and Albert. I could not have written this book without your support and encouragement.

—*Elizabeth Coblentz*

Special thanks to Cathy and Bill Patterson for your meticulous recipe testing and tasting, and to Sharon Fuge and Jessica Alcorn for your time and effort. Thanks also to my wonderful girlfriend, Rachel Diver, for your patience and encouragement, and for serving as a sample reader and supporter. And a final thank you to my parents, Jim and Rita, and my brother, Geoff, for your support throughout my Amish odyssey.

Special thanks also goes to our project editor, Julie Bennett, and the folks at Ten Speed Press for their incredible patience and respect for Amish cultural traditions. Without this sensitivity this project would not have been possible, and the result is a book unparalleled in its authenticity.

—Kevin Williams

Introduction

A weathered, calloused hand directs a plastic ballpoint pen across a piece of lined notebook paper, stringing simple sentences into poignant recollections. It's the plastic pen that seems slightly out of place, as a black-bonnet–clad woman writes by the warm glow of a kerosene lamp. If the pen were a quill, this scene would conjure another century, perhaps a pioneer prairie home in 1850s America or a rustic kitchen in seventeenth-century Switzerland. As I stand by the stove to warm myself, the woman slowly writes, spinning tales from a bygone era, of quilting bees, big family breakfasts, barn raisings, and church dinners.

In the adjoining room, someone is singing a vaguely haunting tune, something between a song and a chant. I can't understand the words, which are sung in Swiss, but I know that I'm listening to a sound from another time and place. Surveying the simple yet comfortable surroundings, I have to remind myself that this is neither the nineteenth century nor a remote Swiss village. This is the year 2001, in the heart of Midwestern Indiana, and the Amish woman writing quietly at her well-worn desk is Elizabeth Coblentz, an unexpected heroine known to thousands of adoring readers across the United States as the Amish Cook.

Since one fateful day in July 1991, when I happened upon the Coblentz's weathered two-story clapboard farmhouse, Elizabeth and I have been partners in an unprecedented writer-editor relationship. Every week Elizabeth sends me the handwritten text for "The Amish Cook," a recipe column that currently appears in more than ninety newspapers across the country. Her uncomplicated descriptions of daily life and meals in an Old Order Amish community come to me by mail because the doctrines of Elizabeth's religion forbid her from owning a telephone, or using a fax machine or computer. I type up Elizabeth's words, make sure the recipes are complete, then publish them for the world to enjoy. With all the modern methods of communication closed to us, the production of a weekly column has been nothing short of a monumental challenge. However, the positive feedback we've received from Elizabeth's numerous fans has made the unusual working arrangement more than worth it.

How It All Began

I was standing in the cluttered but comfortable kitchen of an Amish woman named Catherine Eicher when the idea of an Amish cookery column was born. This was in Reading, Michigan, the land of the Amish, where little changes—ever. Creaking barns tucked into the folds of rolling wheat fields lend a timelessness to this land. In an America where mobility has turned family trees into a tangle of untraceable lineage, the Amish family roots sunk into the soil over a hundred years ago have held fast.

As a junior in an Ohio high school I was assigned a class research project. Each student had to select an item out of the newspaper and write a research paper on it. A small article in *USA Today* captured my interest. It was about a giant chemical corporation seeking a permit to build an incinerator on prime Amish farmland outside of Mansfield, Ohio. I had held a mild interest in the Amish since my teens, when my parents and I stopped at a

roadside cheese stand in Adams County, Ohio. My Dad explained that the bearded man selling homemade cheese out of a buggy was part of a religious group that lives very much like the early American pioneers.

That class assignment started a journey that continues to this day. I submitted my paper to the Ohio state legislature and it became the basis for my first published work: a magazine article in *Environmental Action* magazine. My local newspaper did a story about my article and then offered me a journalism internship for the summer. Soon after, I took an assignment with a Michigan publication to write a story about the state's growing Amish population, which is how I eventually found myself in Catherine Eicher's kitchen.

I had been exploring the tiny grids of criss-crossing country roads when I met Mrs. Eicher, a stout, friendly woman who was cultivating tomatoes, radishes, and rhubarb. She invited me into her kitchen, where kettles and copper pots dangled from hooks in the ceiling and the ever-present smell of rhubarb drifted through the room on a scant breeze. Mrs. Eicher had a small stack of handwritten cookbooks that she sold for a couple of dollars. *Mother's Favorite Recipes* had a blue cardboard cover with flowers on the front, and someone had photocopied the pages and stapled them into book form. I bought one and took it home.

The vision of Catherine Eicher's world—and the charm of that cookbook—stayed with me as I returned to Ohio to write my magazine article. It was 1991, the start of the Internet boom and the last decade of the century. The Amish had stirred something within me. Although they seem anachronistic, they are also vaguely reassuring, a touchstone to a lost era. For me, the Amish represent a living link between a simpler time and today's more chaotic world. They represent one of the last remnants of an agrarian America. I figured that if I had this yearning for something meaningful, then others might be looking for it as well. And just like that, "The Amish Cook" column began to solidify in my mind. Before long, I was headed back to Catherine Eicher's on a mission to persuade her to write a newspaper column.

Searching for the Amish Cook

Leaving at dawn dressed in my best suit, I hit the road for the four-hour trip to Michigan. I figured I'd quickly talk Mrs. Eicher into writing the weekly column, then grab some lunch and make it home by early evening.

When I arrived, Mrs. Eicher gave me a friendly greeting, recognizing me as the young journalist who had visited her a few weeks before. I pitched the idea to her: "I was wondering if you would like to write a weekly newspaper column about your life?" She politely declined. She was too busy with cooking, cleaning, and canning to write such a column.

Undeterred, I stopped by the homes of some of the other Amish women I had met while on assignment for the magazine. All greeted me with polite, but suspicious stares. The Amish are wary of outsiders, whom they refer to as "English" or "Yankees," and I probably appeared to be another huckster trying to lure them into a scheme. Needless to say, they all turned me down as well.

At my last stop a middle-aged Amish man with a long salt-and-pepper-colored beard gave me a small wire-bound cookbook written by an Indiana Amish woman. It was approaching noon and I had no Amish columnist, so I turned my car around and headed two hours south, to the remote Indiana town where the cookbook's author lived. I went to the address I had been given, only to be told that the woman had left the Amish order and moved to Virginia. Strike two.

Feeling disheartened, I decided to give the effort one more hour, then call it quits and head home. I stopped at Amish bakeries and dry goods stores in this rural Indiana outpost, hoping to find a woman who would become the columnist I envisioned when I first saw *Mother's Favorite Recipes.* The same polite, but standoffish refusals greeted me until I spotted two Amish women standing in a driveway and took the chance of turning in.

Meeting the Coblentzes

The Coblentz home is surrounded by pastureland on three sides and a small forest on the fourth. A few apple trees litter the lawn with sweet fruit during the summer. It's an area that has changed little since Swiss settlers began tilling the land here over a century ago. On that midsummer day, I was touched by the sense of history that seemed to permeate the land. I wish I could remember what exactly I said to Elizabeth during that chance first meeting. Her daughters laugh when recalling that day, describing me as "very nervous."

As I stood in Elizabeth's driveway and described to her my vision for a column, I couldn't have known that Elizabeth was already a writer, having contributed letters to *The Budget* for the past forty years. *The Budget* is a subscription newspaper based in Sugarcreek, Ohio, which is circulated throughout Amish communities nationwide. Without telephones or email, the Amish rely on *The Budget* to find out news of their friends and families. Writers known as *scribes* report the news from their communities, chronicling births, deaths, weddings, and anything else of interest. My vision for a column was one that incorporated the same down-home, pioneering spirit as *The Budget*.

Verena and Susan, who were outside in the driveway saying good-bye to Leah after her visit, got a laugh when Kevin first visited us on that warm day in July. We could tell he was nervous. He greeted us with a hearty "Veegates," the traditional Pennsylvania German greeting. He asked me about writing a column, and I guess I thought I would give the task a try. I had been writing for **The Budget** *since I was age sixteen, so this seemed natural. I never thought the column would be in so many papers. I feel unworthy of all the attention from it. It isn't always easy to think of what to write, so I just put my thoughts down on paper.*

Finding a Home for the Amish Cook

After I received Elizabeth's first handwritten column, I put together a crude marketing packet and approached newspaper editors in an attempt to sell the column. One editor in Mansfield, Ohio, looked at my business card and said "Ha, you're an editor? Is your girlfriend your assistant editor? Is this a class assignment?" Another editor, with the *Journal-News* in Hamilton, Ohio, thoughtfully listened to my pitch and studied "The Amish Cook" promotional brochure. I thought that my salesmanship had finally broken through until he whipped out a red pen and began circling spelling errors and grammatical mistakes. He was right—but I was humiliated. (For the record, Mansfield and Hamilton added "The Amish Cook" to their newspapers eight years after that awkward first visit.)

Our original plan for the first column Elizabeth wrote was to simply call the column "The Amish Cook," without Elizabeth's name attached. However, the newspaper editors quickly rejected that idea, so we used Elizabeth's whole name. If I had to do it over again, I would have created a pen name. While I work hard to preserve Elizabeth's privacy, her celebrity does occasionally cause problems that a typical Amish woman wouldn't experience. Sometimes autograph seekers come to her home, and some show up expecting to be fed a home-cooked meal. Like most Amish women, Elizabeth prefers her anonymity.

I started mailing sales packets later that summer, which was the time between my freshman and sophomore years in college. One of these packets caught the eye of Mike Hilfrink, managing editor of the *Quincy Herald-Whig* in Quincy, Illinois. "What made the column unique is that it wasn't just a recipe column. Every week, you got a peek into Amish life and values," Hilfrink told *BusinessWeek* magazine in a 1997 interview.

He decided to try "The Amish Cook," and we had made our first sale. Soon a tiny newspaper in Indiana also subscribed, bringing our total to two newspapers. Today, "The Amish Cook" is in more than a hundred newspapers from coast to coast.

Hard to believe it's been over ten years since Kevin first came here and this column began. How time takes way. The girls always say that Kevin is just like a brother to them, they always say that.

Florists and Carrier Pigeons

Over the past ten years I've had to come up with some creative ways to communicate with Elizabeth. Most editors can pick up the phone and call their columnists if they have a question, say, about how much sugar goes into a Snickerdoodle recipe or what kind of pepper to use in an Amish goulash recipe. I haven't had that luxury. Without phones or electricity, quick methods of communication just aren't possible with the Amish. However, with a combination of long drives, overnight mail, and other creative means, I've managed to communicate with Elizabeth pretty effectively. One time I

called a florist and had a basket of daisies sent to Elizabeth. On the card, I included a message that read "Is it light or dark corn syrup?" The note made for a puzzled florist, but the message got through.

Another time I was inspired by the tales of generals during World War II using carrier pigeons to take messages to the front lines. When I consulted an expert on the possibility of doing the same to communicate with Elizabeth, he said "It's a great idea, except for this to work, you would need to have a colony at her place and at yours." Living in an apartment complex at the time, I envisioned a colony of carrier pigeons on my balcony. I tried to come up with a persuasive pitch to my landlord or an explanation to neighbors about their splattered cars. Nothing seemed plausible, so I abandoned the idea.

When Elizabeth and I set out to produce this cookbook, I knew we'd face a whole new set of unique challenges. One time a draft of our Ten Speed Press editor's revisions blew off Elizabeth's buggy as she drove to her daughter's house, scattering the pages across a soybean field. Most of the manuscript was retrieved, but some farmer in rural Indiana probably ended up harvesting a few chapters.

Most of the book was written and edited through the mail. I sent Elizabeth assignments and she completed them and sent them back. Sometimes she wouldn't provide quite enough detail, so I would have to mail her to tell her to send me revisions. This constant snail-mailing stretched the work out over a period of two years. Eventually I realized that some modern technology would be needed if we wanted the book released in this century.

I ended up renting a hotel suite not far from Elizabeth's home. I carted my computer to the hotel, then brought Elizabeth and her daughters Susan and Verena there for the day. Since I was

The Coblentz Family

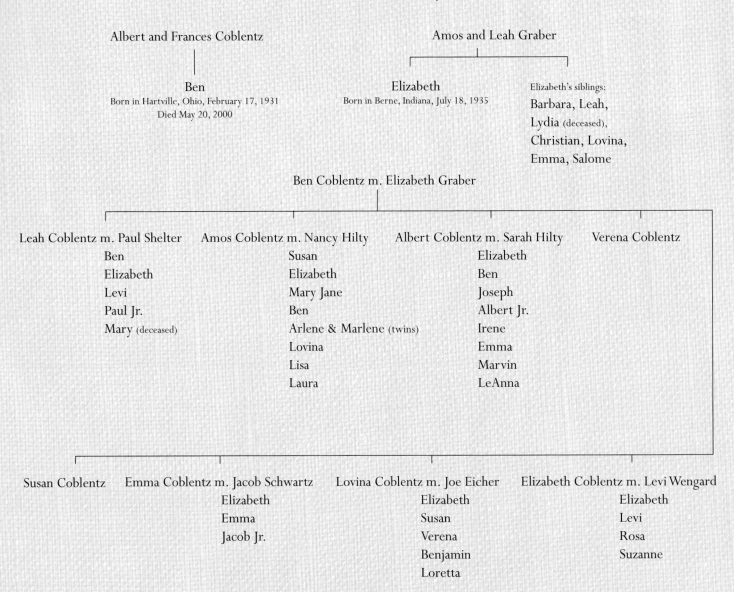

Albert and Frances Coblentz

Ben
Born in Hartville, Ohio, February 17, 1931
Died May 20, 2000

Amos and Leah Graber

Elizabeth
Born in Berne, Indiana, July 18, 1935

Elizabeth's siblings:
Barbara, Leah,
Lydia (deceased),
Christian, Lovina,
Emma, Salome

Ben Coblentz m. Elizabeth Graber

Leah Coblentz m. Paul Shelter
Ben
Elizabeth
Levi
Paul Jr.
Mary (deceased)

Amos Coblentz m. Nancy Hilty
Susan
Elizabeth
Mary Jane
Ben
Arlene & Marlene (twins)
Lovina
Lisa
Laura

Albert Coblentz m. Sarah Hilty
Elizabeth
Ben
Joseph
Albert Jr.
Irene
Emma
Marvin
LeAnna

Verena Coblentz

Susan Coblentz

Emma Coblentz m. Jacob Schwartz
Elizabeth
Emma
Jacob Jr.

Lovina Coblentz m. Joe Eicher
Elizabeth
Susan
Verena
Benjamin
Loretta

Elizabeth Coblentz m. Levi Wengard
Elizabeth
Levi
Rosa
Suzanne

going to be away from home for a few days, I also brought my dog, Kira, with me.

So Elizabeth wouldn't come in contact with my computer, a possible violation of her religious beliefs, she sat in a chair near me while I sat at my keyboard. I asked her questions interview-style, and she supplied the answers for the book. Because Elizabeth's column is very popular in the town we were in, I used a private entrance to the hotel so no one would see her arrive. Anyone who used the back stairwell at the Holiday Inn Express in Celina, Ohio, would have thought it a strange sight to run into me carrying a German Shepherd and a computer, followed by three Amish women.

This cookbook is the culmination of a decade's worth of hard work. The unique professional arrangement between Elizabeth and me has not always been an easy one. There were times when I struggled to pay Elizabeth at the end of the month, when overeager readers invaded her precious privacy, and when the demands of writing a weekly column caused Elizabeth to consider giving it up. But Ben always managed to motivate her to keep soldiering forward. Elizabeth told me recently, as this cookbook was nearing completion, that Ben must have seen the future. For Elizabeth, this book is a validation of Ben's vision.

For me, this cookbook represents the conclusion of a journey that began in high school. Over the past ten years, the Coblentzes have become family. We've transcended the cultural chasm between us in a rare way and I'm able to view the Amish culture from a more realistic standpoint. The Amish are just like everyone else—with their frailties and flaws—but I've learned a lot from Elizabeth and the people of her community. My hope for this cookbook is that it will encourage others to appreciate the struggles of our ancestors, to recognize the importance of family, and to slow down and savor life's simplicities.

A History of the Amish

The Amish derive their name from their spiritual founder, Jacob Amman of Switzerland, who, with a group of followers, separated from the nascent Mennonite movement in 1693, believing the Mennonites had become too liberal. The Mennonites were part of a larger religious revolt against Catholicism known as Anabaptism (for the practice of baptising followers during adulthood, rather than infancy), which was gaining ground in the fifteenth and sixteenth centuries.

Sometimes referred to as "Pennsylvania Dutch," the Amish (along with the Mennonites, Dunkers, and Quakers) aren't Dutch at all. Because the Amish speak a dialect of Swiss-German, they came to be called "Pennsylvania Deutsche" (which means "Pennsylvania German") after their immigration to America. Because the word *Deutsche* looked and sounded like the word *Dutch* to early Americans, the Amish came to be called "Pennsylvania Dutch." The Pennsylvania German are also sometimes called "Plain People," a name that refers to their avoidance of all things fancy or ornate.

Amish culture is based on *Gelassenheit,* a German word that means "submission to authority." Although *Gelassenheit* is not a word most Amish use frequently, it is constantly manifested in several ways. Amish personalities are reserved, modest, calm, and quiet. The Amish value submission, pacifism, obedience to God and their church, humility in demeanor, and simplicity in lifestyle. Their rituals include adult baptism, the confession of sins, the ordination of lay ministers (there are no professional clergy), and foot washing. Their social structure is small, informal, local, and decentralized.

The Amish reject most modern technology, but not all. Some might find the Amish selection of which technology they use and which they reject to be baffling, maybe even hypocritical, but to the Amish their choices make perfect sense. For instance, the Amish are not permitted to own automobiles, but they are allowed to ride in cars owned by non-Amish individuals for travel to faraway funerals or for important errands. The Amish make similar provisions with telephones. They may sometimes use them to conduct important business or make contact with a relative, but none are allowed inside the home. It's not the technology that the Amish reject, it's the baggage the technology brings. A phone in the home would open their ideological isolation to continual invasion from the outside world. Using a public phone is okay, but a quiet family

The largest Old Order Amish population lives in the peaceful hills of Holmes County, Ohio, with about twenty-five thousand Amish. The Amish church has more than a hundred thousand members in the United States and Canada.

Amish Buggies

We have the open, horse-drawn buggies in our community. Some areas have the covered buggies, or what is called a "top buggy." Top buggies are enclosed and probably have no blankets inside to dry afterwards when it's raining, snowing, or whatever. We use an umbrella to protect us from getting wet. In the wintertime, the umbrella really holds off the cold wind.

We have a license plate for each buggy. The slow-moving triangle emblem is also on the back end of the buggy along with reflectors of various colors. Most buggies have two blinkers and some have the flashers. It pays to be well-lighted on these busy roads.

The buggy consists of one long seat when the family is small. Some have two and three seats on a buggy when there's a larger family. We still usually own a one-seater for when the whole family doesn't go somewhere. Years ago, we used to have string seats on our buggies, but not many are seen with string seats anymore.

evening could easily be interrupted by the jangling ring of a phone if one were permitted in the home. The Amish don't completely reject technology, they just keep it at arm's length. In fact, the Amish have had a progressive history when it comes to new technologies, having invented the Conestoga wagon, which helped settle the American West; a popular musket; and efficient farming techniques that are still copied to this day.

The day-to-day lives of the Amish are governed by the *Ordnung*, a set of unwritten rules that outlines how a community lives, from the type of clothing permitted to the type of reflectors used on their buggies. *Ordnung* varies from community to community, but variations are usually minor. The Amish in Seymour, Missouri, for instance, are not allowed to have roofs on their horse-drawn buggies, while the Amish in northern Indiana are permitted to have roofs and even rubber wheels. To enforce the doctrines of their religion, most Amish communities still practice *meidung* (shunning). Often a tool of last resort, this practice allows the Amish to permanently banish a person who strays from religious teachings.

Amish communities can be found in nineteen U.S. states and Ontario, Canada. The vast majority, however, live in Pennsylvania, Indiana, and Ohio. In the early eighteenth century, William Penn opened up Pennsylvania as a haven for religious orders. This was appealing to the Amish, who had been persecuted in Europe for

> **The oldest, continually used hymnal among the Pennsylvania German, or among any religion for that matter, is used by the Amish. The *Ausbund* dates back to 1564 and first appeared in Switzerland.**

their pacifist beliefs. There are stories of Amish who were tied into burlap sacks and tossed into rivers, burned alive, or forced into hiding. When word began circulating that William Penn was promising a land of religious freedom, the Amish packed their belongings and headed to America, with the first waves arriving in the 1730s. The following accounts of Elizabeth's ancestor's journeys to America were culled from diaries and oral stories passed down through the generations of her family.

I often think how nice we have it now, to think how my great-great-grandfather from Santiglet, Department Dauchs, France, came to America. His conscientious objection to compulsory military training in France was behind his decision to immigrate to the New World. It sure must've been sad for his family to leave behind their friends, loved ones, neighbors, and all the scenes of their childhood, to move to a land unknown more than three thousand miles away across the wild and stormy deep.

They made the trip in five months; it could now be made in hours by airplane. When they boarded the ship, they didn't step onto a luxurious ocean liner as we see today. Conditions aboard the ship were anything but agreeable. It was a different life in Europe. Their cooking was quite simple compared to ours now. Lots of their food was dried. The edibles taken on board were not very good and not any too plentiful. Meat was salted and packed in barrels, and even then some of it spoiled en route. Many kegs of drinking water were taken aboard. Bread kept best after it was double-toasted.

Living quarters became extremely crowded, and sleeping conditions were very poor as well as rather unhealthful. They did not have the proper food and sanitation facilities, so sickness became prevalent. It would not be unusual if 10 percent of the people on board a ship from Europe to America would die. When they encountered storms at sea, the ship tossed and rolled furiously, but there was a railing all around the deck to guard passengers from falling into the sea. These storms sometimes lasted two or three days causing plenty of confusion, anxiety, suffering, and seasickness.

It was always impossible to walk the boat when such storms occurred, and it often upset tables and rolled the seasick passengers from their berths. The massive sails were often tossed about like feathers, and broken masts and torn sails had to be repaired before the ship could continue on its hazardous journey. There wasn't a weather bureau like today, which could've aided the sailors to steer clear of storms, nor aids to carry messages to the ship.

The ancestors on my mother's side also had a tough time. They were Mennonite fugitives from Bern, Switzerland. They went to Alsace, France, during the last half of the seventeenth century and established themselves in the county of Rebeau Pierre, near Sainte-Marie-aux-Mines. However, they were driven out from there in 1712 by the order of Louis XIV, king of France. They traveled northward and located in the township of Montbéliard, which, at the time, was part of the Empire of Germany known as Duchide-Wartemburg. Our ancestors were among a group of Mennonite families who settled in that part of Germany in 1793. They had purchased a large farm in Monte-pre-Voir Township of the Nevier District of Monte-be-Laird.

Elizabeth's mother's ancestors would eventually be chased out of Germany and would also head to the United States. The Amish found Pennsylvania's Lancaster County to be reminiscent of the land they left behind and so happily settled their families there or in neighboring states. Today, there are no Amish left in Europe.

A Day in the Life

Some ask what a typical day in this household is like. The only good answer is that every day is different! We get up about 4:00 A.M. each morning. No alarm clock is needed; we just rise at that time. Naturally my day-to-day duties have changed somewhat from when I had eight children living under my care to now, when it is just me, Susan, and Verena at home. When my children were small there was lots more laundry to do, food to cook, and dinners to prepare. Following is a diary for a day in July 1996, shortly after Emma and Jacob were united in marriage and living here with Ben and I.

4:00 A.M. Time to get up on this nice, breezy morning. Ben and Jacob go out to hand-milk our five cows and do the rest of the barn work (feeding the cows, feeding the horses, etc). Emma and I start breakfast, with the assistance of Susan. Verena gets herself ready to leave for the sewing factory in town.

4:50 A.M. We're all seated at the table to feast on breakfast, which consists of fried eggs and potatoes, scrambled eggs, coffee soup and crackers, cheese, toast, hot peppers, jam, hot pepper butter, butter, fresh strawberries, coffee, and tea.

5:00 A.M. Jacob leaves for his construction work.

5:30 A.M. Verena leaves for the sewing factory and Ben leaves for his construction work. Ben has been with that company for thirty-seven years. Verena has been at the sewing factory over twelve years now. Verena got a splinter stuck in the top of her foot while visiting at Amos's house on Sunday evening. Ben and I worked so hard to get it removed. But it is stuck in some way. Hard to remove. Hopefully we got it all out. We soaked her foot every morning and evening with Epsom salts and peroxide water. And we are keeping it wrapped with a pulling salve. Emma and Susan are washing the dishes, and will soon hike out to the garden to hoe. I want to put some more sweet corn and hot peppers in the ground.

6:30 A.M. Emma is ironing and Susan helps me put out sweet corn and eighteen hot pepper plants.

7:30 A.M. *We all get cleaned up to go help Liz clean up from their church services on Sunday, which were held in their home. Always plenty to clean up afterwards. Susan runs out to prepare our horse and buggy for the five-mile ride to Liz's.*

8:00 A.M. *We go to Liz's house. Along the way we stop to pick up Lovina in her new home, and her two children. Lovina and Joe just moved to a new home about two miles away from our house.*

8:30 A.M. *We surprise Liz by showing up to help her clean. She is pleasantly surprised!*

2:30 P.M. *After spending the day helping Liz, we head home. We did a huge amount of laundry, cleaned and mopped the floors, washed and rewashed lots of dishes. Was an enjoyable workday together. She was so glad to see almost everything back in order. They had 135 there for supper Sunday evening. We did lots of singing and yodeling as we cleaned, and stopped for a dinner break.*

3:00 P.M. *Verena gets home from the sewing factory.*

4:30 P.M. *Verena prepares a covered skillet casserole for our evening meal. She put a pound of ground beef in a skillet, added a diced-up onion, potatoes that were put through the hand-cranked salad maker, and a can of cream of mushroom soup on top, then topped it with cheese. It takes an hour in the skillet until it is done.*

5:30 P.M. *Ben and Jacob get home from work and go out to do chores, such as milking the cows, feeding the bull and the horses, and cleaning out the barn.*

7:00 P.M. *Verena's casserole was good! Albert and some of Jacob's friends gave us a visit tonight after dinner, so we had a nice evening of visiting. Yesterday, Liz, Lovina, Verena, Susan, and I were at Leah's to help them pack. They are moving to their new home next week, which will bring them lots closer to us (only one and a half miles).*

9:00 P.M. *Evening prayers are said and everyone is ready for a good night's sleep!*

The Recipes

The Amish diet has not changed much throughout their existence in the United States. Since they are primarily farmers, they have been almost entirely self-sufficient, with bountiful gardens, crops, and livestock. However, as occupations and the sociological structure of the Amish began to change in the early 1970s, so, too, did Amish eating habits.

Over the past thirty years, the Amish have begun to venture into grocery stores to buy more processed, modern foods like chips, tuna, and soft drinks. Most of the Amish drink soda and eat chips with their meals. Such changes have resulted in some unusual accommodations, like one Indiana town where, until recently, the Amish bishop forbade church members from going to grocery stores where electronic price scanners were used. So the Amish went to a store that had only manual cash registers. That store eventually closed down, leaving only one grocery store in town, which forced the bishop to adjust his edict.

Amish foods, which for years remained plain, are being spiced up in some communities. The Coblentz family was recently introduced to hot peppers, which Elizabeth laughingly calls "addictive." Simple and spicy is now popular in the Coblentz household, as Elizabeth invents new ways to use these fiery delicacies. Pizza has also slowly crept into the Amish diet. Since the Amish don't have telephones to call for pizza delivery, they have to improvise by making their own. Amish pizzas, which are baked in wood-fired ovens

and tailored to each family's tastes, are delicious with homemade crusts, fresh toppings, and innovative ingredients.

It may be a surprise to learn that the Amish have incorporated other modern foods into their cooking culture. Evidence of this can be found throughout this cookbook, with the use of packaged goods like Jell-O and marshmallows. Although sometimes a recipe will call for a can of soup or a package of noodles, we've also included recipes for homemade soup and noodles when appropriate. We have tried to include only the most traditional, culturally unique Amish recipes, like Shoo-Fly Pie (see page 128), which was a staple on the long journey to the New World.

Because Elizabeth doesn't have electricity, her methods of preparing and storing food are quite different from ours. She has wood and kerosene stoves instead of an oven, and an icebox instead

The Amish have the same silverware sets that most Americans have: china for special occasions, a set of family-style dishes for casual eating, and a supply of paper plates for lazy days. Tupperware is a common sight in Amish kitchens, and an abundance of Mason jars are always on hand for quick canning.

of a refrigerator or freezer. Fruits and vegetables from her garden are canned or frozen for the winter, so when Elizabeth calls for frozen food, she's referring to the farm-fresh products she has stored in the cellar, not to packages plucked from the frozen food section of a market. With eight children and scores of grandchildren, Elizabeth is used to preparing meals for large groups of people. However, all of the recipes included here have been scaled down to a conventional number of servings, and adapted to fit modern kitchens and appliances.

When Ben and I first got married, we bought a farm which had no basement. Ben cut a fifty-gallon wooden barrel in half and put it in the ground. He made a lid for it and there's where the leftover food went. It felt quite cool, but I know meat from the store wouldn't keep too long there. At home, Mother would have a bucket of cold water to help the milk not to sour. Every once in a while on, hot muggy days, the milk would sour by evening. On days like these we would have to change the water to keep the milk in the jar cold. Now, big ice chests and ice boxes are in use, and some use old, deep freezers.

This book is divided into five parts: breakfast, dinner, supper, desserts, and Sundays and special occasions. The three main meals are important benchmarks in the day-to-day lives of the Amish. Meals are the time that these industrious people take a breather to gather with their families for food and fellowship. Desserts are decadent indulgences among the Amish and provide a pleasant ending to a hearty meal, so a chapter has been devoted just to these sweet treats. And the special occasions that mark the Amish year have their own unique menus, like Raisin Pie (see page 153) and Amish Wedding Nothings (see page 148).

The recipes in this book have been passed down to me from my mother, my grandmother, other relatives, and friends. I tried to select the most simple, nourishing recipes that provide the best day-to-day picture of what we eat in this household. Some recipes are timesaving, and some recipes will take longer to prepare. Most of these recipes will be more economical than store-bought items because many of the ingredients are ones you probably already have in your pantry.

Many older people who lived through the Great Depression of the 1930s will recall when the dollar didn't go far. Meals had to be very simple, but nourishing. The Great Depression was a big influence on my mother's cooking. Many of our meals were simple soups: Pennsylvania Pot Pie Soup (see page 81), Winter's Day Chili Soup (see page 64), bean, or tomato soup. And I remember Mother making a delicious brown gravy soup. During the summer months when the berries were ripe, we would have a soup of cold milk and sugar poured over crumbled bread and berries. On a hot day, this cold soup would be our dinner. It was usually strawberries, but mulberries at times also. I also remember Mother making Knepfle (see page 83) and German Rivvel Soup (see page 84). She'd have a soft dough of flour, egg, salt, and water. In boiling broth she'd cut the dough piece by piece with a knife and drop it in to cook awhile till done. Later on, beef and noodles or chicken and noodles were on the menu. We grew up with these simple soups.

Some of these recipes are just passed through our community. I share recipes with other women in the area, and in return, I receive new recipes. The Breakfast Casserole (see page 29), for instance, is a recipe that was given to me by a friend years ago. It is an easy dish to prepare for breakfast and feeds quite a few people; it's become a family favorite.

My daughters use a lot of the recipes that I have passed on to them, so they can prepare them for their families. At times they will come up with new recipes and share them with me. All my daughters enjoy cooking.

Wood and kerosene stoves are the usual scene in my kitchen. I usually use the wood cookstove during the winter and I use the kerosene stove year-round. There's no microwave, dishwasher, or any of the other usual kitchen appliances you might find, as we have no electricity. So there's no electric food processor or whatever. We use hand-operated kitchen utensils, such as the potato masher, and the salad maker, which grates up our vegetables very fine. Stainless-steel cookware is my favorite to use.

Fellowship and Food

My great-grandmother came to America on a ship from Italy around 1900 to begin a new life in America. A century later, the smell of spaghetti sauce bubbling up from an iron kettle on my grandmother's stove tells the tale of Italian immigrants, stretching from the olive groves and vineyards of southern Italy. There's a story in the sauce, of courage and culture and the perseverance to plant new roots in a new land. Food comforts, soothes, and nurtures. Long perfected recipes—soups and stews made with the loving hands of a mother, grandmother, or great-grandmother—reach across continents, oceans, and generations.

The Amish have their own food and their own way of life, forged through centuries of persecution and prayer. The first time I tasted Pennsylvania German food was after a Sunday church service in the home of a German Baptist couple. The food served was true to the tradition of Pennsylvania German cooking: simple, yet elegant. There were gently glazed fillets of farm-fresh chicken, steaming pots of fresh vegetables, sliced homemade bread, and plenty of scratch-made pies and cakes for dessert. The table conversation was full of hearty laughter and warmth.

It would be another two years before I tasted this type of food again. It was at the Coblentz home, when Elizabeth invited me to supper and to listen to the family yodel one evening soon after I first met her. The food was simple, bearing the basic elements of Pennsylvania German cooking, and the music was fascinating, more yodel than chant, with a touch of Swiss. That night and that meal hold a special place in my memory for the abundance of tasty food, good cheer, and family warmth. Elizabeth and I hope the recipes in this book will help you create similar memories in your home with your own family. Enjoy!

CHAPTER 1

Breakfast

Mornings haven't changed much since I was a girl. When I was a young child in my dad and mother's household, we always had Coffee Soup (see page 38), fried potatoes, and cheese in the mornings. Coffee Soup is a mixture of coffee, cream, sugar, and toasted bread. Some people like it sweet, but you can make it to your taste.

When I was a girl, eggs were hardly ever fried. We always just scrambled them—I think because we thought it was healthier. I remember when I had the measles as a teenager that my mother asked me if I would like an egg for breakfast. I was not hungry for anything because I was so sick. Then when I recovered, I wished I had an egg, but they were not always plentiful in those days. We hardly ever had bacon or ham for breakfast. It was just more simple back then. Mother would cook cornmeal in the evening and let it set overnight because my dad liked his Fried Cornmeal Mush (see page 32) in the morning.

There was always a lot of work to do before breakfast. I remember hanging the laundry up by lantern light before going to work at a produce company when I was a teenager. And after Ben and I were married and had started a family, mornings became even more a time of hustle and bustle, especially when all of our children were still living at home. We would wake up at 4:00 A.M. with plenty of chores awaiting us, and then have a good, hearty breakfast before the menfolk headed out to work. Everybody got up at the same time and ate breakfast together. Some of the children would go out to milk the cows, and some of them would help prepare breakfast. At one time, we had twelve cows that needed milking every day. Our sons, Amos and Albert, both started milking at age five. We had a big stainless-steel strainer on top of the milk cans. The boys would pour the milk into the strainer to strain it, and a milk hauler would come to take the milk away. Amos always wanted to help Ben with the milking.

Breakfast is a busy time, but it's also a quiet time for the family to be together before going their separate ways for the day and a time to listen to the songs of the early morning birds. The sun is usually rising during breakfast and the smell

A POEM FROM
ELIZABETH'S CHILDHOOD

A boy of three, a girl of four,
Were playing house one day,
They played that they were man
and wife,
And they were going away.
They knocked upon the neighbor's door,
The little girl bowed low,
"This is my husband; I'm his wife
We're visiting, you know."
"Come in, come in" the lady said
"And take yourself a seat,
I'll bring you both some lemonade
And something good to eat."
She gave them each a big tall glass
A cookie and a plate,
She offered them a second cup
Of fresh lemonade.
"Oh no, thank you," the wee lass said
As she took the small boy's hand:
"We really have to go now,
my husband wet his pants."

Author Unknown

of fried eggs and potatoes is in the air. It's so nice to see the sunrise. We would have a silent prayer at the breakfast table and then Ben would lead a prayer after breakfast. A perfect way to begin the day. After breakfast, some of the girls packed dinners for the men, some made beds, while others mopped the floors. There was always lots of activity around here in the mornings. Even though my children have grown up and moved out, nowadays there are grandchildren here visiting, so breakfast still needs to be made.

On weekends or holidays, the pace is slower. Once a year, for our Christmas gathering, we have the whole family over for a big breakfast and a whole-day get-together. It's always so good to have the family together. At such a time the kitchen is filled with the aroma of from-scratch cinnamon rolls from the oven or cooked apples on the range. Homemade biscuits are a favorite. We prepare around sixty eggs in the morning when the whole family comes and I make a couple of loaves of homemade bread. By next year maybe it will take even more eggs. I enjoy having the whole family in for the morning meal and am going to do it as long as I'm able.

The Lord's Prayer

This is our Lord's Prayer, which we begin most of our meals with. It is said in Pennsylvania German in our home. Many of you might not understand it, but some who know German (and even those who don't), might find it interesting to look at.

> Unser vater der du bist im himmel,
> geheiliget werde dein name zu komme
> uns dein reich, dein ville geschehe auf
> erden vie im himmel, gib uns heit.
> unser täglich brod, under vergib uns
> unsere schuld, vie wir vergeben
> unsern schuldern; und las uns nicht
> eingeführt werden in verschung,
> sondern erlöse uns von dem bösen;
> denn dein ist das reich, dein ist die
> kraft, dein ist die herrlichkeit in weigkeit.
> Umen.

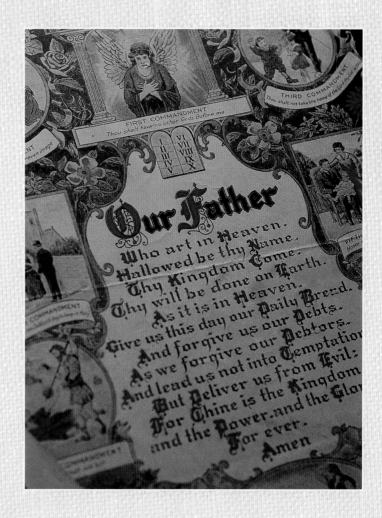

The Amish Cook

by Elizabeth Coblentz

March 1992

All around us, tints of green begin coloring the drab landscape. Tiny green leaves deck the stark brown branches. In the ground, seeds and roots enliven with growth. Beautiful buds and blooms and flowers will come forth. Bright reds and yellows, sharp blues, deep and pale pinks, deep and pale purples, and pure whites. Very delicately are they formed and very pleasing are they to behold.

Housecleaning time again. How good to push up the windows and let the fresh air come in. An inner force impels us to be energetic.

Tomorrow, March 11, it'll be thirty-four years since Ben and I took up on housekeeping. So it was quite a change after working at the nearby produce factory for quite some years. Butchering chickens was among my duties. The produce plant is a thing of the past now.

On March 12, 1948, the temperature was 7 degrees below, and then in March, 1986, we had a record high of 82 degrees. But I still planted onions, radishes, and lettuce. Not much of each. The ground was dry enough to plant more but I don't like to replant. Too early for me.

We had three thunderstorms last month, which was very unusual in this area. There's usually no thunderstorms this time of year. It's been a dreary month. It was a rainy morning, but has turned to snow now.

Doughnuts

Makes about 24 doughnuts

4 1/4 cups plus 1/4 cup all-purpose flour
1/4 teaspoon salt
3 teaspoons baking powder
1 cup sugar
1 cup milk
2 tablespoons butter (softened)
2 eggs
1/2 teaspoon vanilla
3 pounds shortening or 1 (48-ounce bottle) oil for frying
1 cup sugar for dusting (optional)
2 teaspoons ground cinnamon for dusting (optional)
1 cup powdered sugar for dusting (optional)

In a large bowl, sift together 4 1/4 cups of the flour, the salt, and the baking powder. Add the sugar and set aside. In a medium bowl, stir together the milk, butter, eggs, and vanilla until creamy. Make a well in the center of the flour mixture and pour the milk mixture into the well. Work the flour into the milk mixture until you have a soft dough that is easy to handle and not sticky.

Spread the remaining flour over a flat rolling surface. Turn the dough onto the rolling surface, sprinkling some of the flour over the dough so it doesn't stick to the rolling pin. Roll out the dough to approximately 3/8 inch thick. Using the rim of a drinking glass or a doughnut cutter, cut out 3-inch rounds. With doughnut-hole cutters or a knife, make a 2-inch hole in the center of each round (smaller holes can be made, but they will close during frying). Store the uncooked doughnuts in the refrigerator until you are ready to fry them; they'll be easier to handle. In a deep pan, melt the shortening for frying. When the shortening reaches 365° (or when a piece of dough dropped into the pan sizzles), drop the doughnuts into the pan and fry for 2 minutes on each side. Remove the doughnuts and allow to drain on a paper towel.

In a bowl, mix together the sugar and cinnamon. Place the powdered sugar in a separate bowl. While the doughnuts are still warm, roll them in the sugar-cinnamon mixture or the powdered sugar to your taste.

The main ingredient in this recipe is home-processed sausage (see page 72). Once a year we butcher our hogs, which gives us our supply of sausage, ham, and bacon. Not all sausage is the same. If you want to make a high-quality sausage, put ham in the mix before putting it through the grinder. We also add a little ground beef. The men's job is to trim the meat off from the bones. I don't like the link sausage, but some of our kids do links. Ben and I always did bulk sausage. Some people in our community add garlic and a lot of other spices, but we never preferred it.

This dish is so easy and quick to prepare, and nutritious too. We made four pans full on New Year's Day of 2000, for our annual family Christmas gathering. Four eight-foot tables were used to seat the entire family, a total of forty-five people. One pan of Breakfast Casserole was placed on each table. We also served fried potatoes, ham, bacon, cheese, toast, and leftover Christmas goodies like cookies, fruitcakes, and pumpkin rolls.

Breakfast Casserole

8 slices white or wheat bread, crumbled

6 eggs

2 cups milk

1 onion, diced

1/2 teaspoon salt

1/2 teaspoon dry mustard

1 pound crumbled bulk sausage, fried and drained

1 pound grated Colby cheese

1/4 cup margarine or butter

Preheat the oven to 325°. Put the bread in the bottom of a greased 9 by 13-inch baking dish. In a separate bowl, beat the eggs, then add the milk, onion, salt, and mustard. Sprinkle the sausage and cheese over the bread. Dot the margarine over the cheese and pour the egg mixture over all. Bake for 45 minutes to 1 hour, until golden brown.

The New Year's Song was brought over from Switzerland and has been sung in my family ever since. On New Year's Day, the young people, sometimes in up to twenty horse-drawn buggies, will stop from house to house to sing the New Year's Song. It is sung in German: "Die Zeit Ist Ankummen das fried" are the first words. The song roughly translates into: "The time has come for the New Year, God will give us a good New Year." There are several variations of the song.

This cooked oatmeal is good and hearty to eat with any other foods on the breakfast menu, and it's easy to make. On those mornings we don't know what to eat for breakfast, we usually say "So, what about oatmeal?" Ben never liked milk in his oatmeal so I cook it in water. For those who like milk with it, just add some. I add a little salt to the water to give the oatmeal a better flavor, and I also add some brown sugar. I like my oatmeal when it turns thicker. The size of the cooking pot depends on how many people will be joining us for breakfast. For this recipe, use a 1-quart kettle. We usually eat oatmeal with fried eggs and potatoes.

Winter Morning Oatmeal

Serves 4

2 cups old-fashioned oatmeal

1/8 teaspoon salt

1 teaspoon brown sugar

Boil 2 cups of water in a 1-quart kettle or saucepan. Add the oatmeal, salt, and sugar. Cook for several minutes over medium heat, stirring from time to time. You'll know it's done when it has a thick, paste-like consistency. Serve hot.

Since the day of her marriage to Ben, Elizabeth has referred to herself as Mrs. Ben Coblentz. Amish women are traditionally deferential to the men in their families, addressing themselves and each other by their husband's name. This practice also extends to casual conversation. For instance, when Elizabeth refers to one of her children's families, she uses the name of the husband to mean the whole family. Daughter Lovina is married to Joe, so Elizabeth will refer to their family as "Joe's." When talking about her son Albert's family, she says "Albert's," which, again, refers to the whole family.

If we ran out of bread when I was grow-ing up, we made some biscuits. Some homemade butter would also be pre-pared. Homemade butter wasn't hard to make. Mother just put the cream in a quart jar and shook it and shook it until it got thick. The thick part was a very spreadable, homemade butter and the liquid part was buttermilk, which could then be used to make Buttermilk Cookies (see page 121). When I make homemade butter with my own family, I sometimes add a little salt and some yellow cake coloring to make it more yellow. Home-made butter doesn't keep so long; it gets moldy sooner than the boughten kind. I put homemade butter in a different con-tainer and store it in the ice chest.

Biscuits have always been a favorite part of the morning meal. Some people make sausage gravy to top the hot bis-cuits, but I usually make gravy with milk. When cooked, I season it with salt and pepper to taste, and add a small amount of butter or margarine. I usually make milk gravy and biscuits when our adult children come home for a morning meal. I prepare fried eggs and potatoes along with it for the big eaters in the family, who enjoy something else to eat with their biscuits.

Breakfast Biscuits with Homemade Milk Gravy

Makes 12 (3-inch-round) biscuits and 4 cups gravy

BISCUITS

2 cups all-purpose flour

1 tablespoon baking powder

1 teaspoon salt

1/4 cup Homemade Mayonnaise (see page 167) or store-bought mayonnaise

1 cup milk

1 teaspoon sugar

GRAVY

2 quarts plus 3 tablespoons milk

3 tablespoons all-purpose flour

1 teaspoon margarine or butter

Salt

Pepper

Preheat the oven to 375°. To make the bis-cuits, in a large bowl, sift together the flour, baking powder, and salt. Add the mayonnaise, milk, and sugar and mix with a spoon for 2 to 3 minutes, until you have a smooth and soft white dough. The dough will be slightly sticky. Using a lightly floured tablespoon, drop the dough onto a greased 11 by 7-inch cookie sheet or fill twelve greased muffin tins two-thirds full. When baked on a cookie sheet, the batter will spread out during bak-ing. Bake for 18 to 20 minutes. When the bis-cuits are done, they will be a light, golden brown in color, about 3 inches wide and 1 inch tall, with a light and fluffy texture.

To make the gravy, in a small bowl, mix the 3 tablespoons of milk with the flour until smooth. Heat the 2 quarts of milk in a 10-inch skillet. When the milk is hot but not boiling, add the milk and flour mixture. Mixing the milk and flour together ahead of time means no lumps in your gravy. Add the margarine. Season with salt and pepper to your taste. Stir over medium heat till thickened. The gravy will be very light in color. Serve hot over the biscuits.

This meal isn't always just for breakfast. I can remember my mother cooking mush for the evening meal. She liked to have a cup of milk in one hand and by spoon she'd dip the mush in the milk and eat it. I didn't care for the cooked mush that way, but I liked it when fried in the morning.

I cook our cornmeal mush the evening before, then put it in a loaf pan to give it shape, and place it in our cellar overnight, where it is dark and cool. A modern, electric refrigerator should work just as well. In the morning, I slice the cornmeal into pieces. You can slice thick or thin pieces, however you prefer. We put maple syrup or molasses, honey, or apple butter on top of the fried mush. It is very nourishing.

Fried Cornmeal Mush

Serves 4 to 6

4 cups water

1 cup white cornmeal

1 teaspoon salt

2 tablespoons cooking oil

Maple syrup (optional)

Bring 3 cups of the water to a boil in a large saucepan. In a separate bowl, make a thickening with the cornmeal, salt, and the remaining 1 cup of water. The mixture will be very thick and grainy. Add this mixture to the boiling water and stir until it reaches the boiling point again. The mixture will still be grainy. Cook for 15 to 20 minutes, stirring occasionally, until the mush is very thick. Pour the mixture into an 8 by 5-inch loaf pan and cover and cool overnight in the refrigerator.

To fry, heat the oil in a skillet over medium heat. Slice the chilled cornmeal into 1-inch-thick pieces and fry for 5 minutes on each side, until golden brown. For an even better taste, lightly drizzle maple syrup over the slices before eating.

Hint: Unused portions of the cornmeal mixture can be stored in the refrigerator for several days.

Traditional Amish Morning Meals

Liver Pudding and Pon Hoss are considered delicacies among the Amish. Although most non-Amish cooks aren't equipped to prepare them, these two dishes provide a fascinating peek into the world of the Amish and their legendary self-sufficiency.

CANNED LIVER PUDDING

Liver pudding is an old recipe, made while butchering pork. It comes from the head meat and the bones, which are cooked soft in an iron kettle. The meat goes through a grinder and gets mixed up. We usually put ours in jars right away and process it, though some of the area Amish put it in an iron kettle to fry it down a little before putting it into jars to process. In that way, it is more like a sausage. I always like liver pudding with coffee soup and fried potatoes. Ben used to like liver pudding with fried potatoes topped with applesauce.

When Ben and I were first married, we would have liver pudding for supper. Meat wasn't plentiful because we couldn't afford to buy it and we didn't have hogs to butcher on our own. One time Ben and I went into town and he only had twenty-seven cents left in his pocket; but we still lived happily and we had plenty to eat. We lived on the next road over, and had a five-room home with no upstairs and no basement. I stored my canned goods in the back room. When winter came the canned goods froze, and some of the cans busted. We moved to our present location in 1963.

I remember Ben working on those cold days. He would come home in the evening and be so cold. It was such a cold little house. We put the table beside the wood-burning stove in the living room and put our baby Leah on it. In the bedroom you could hear the steam coming out of the stove. We cuddled her between us and tried to keep her warm. I don't think the children nowadays know what we went through.

PON HOSS

Pon Hoss is made with the juice that's left from the pork bones that have been cooked in the iron kettle. It is made with a thickening of flour or cornmeal and some liver pudding. We season it with salt and pepper. After it is cooked and thickened in the iron kettle, it is put into loaf pans to chill. When it's chilled, we cut it into slices and fry it in a skillet till golden brown. The age of the hog determines whether the pon hoss is moist or dry. If it's not moist, we add a little lard. We like ours sliced on the thin side. Some people put it into jars and process it for later on. It's yummy to have with coffee soup.

The Amish Cook

by Elizabeth Coblentz

July 1992

Friendly greetings to all you readers across the miles. Another day has come and has almost ended. One half of 1992 is now history. Time sure keeps moving along at a brisk pace. This summer was almost a perfect growing season till the rains came. The ground is well soaked. Thousands and thousands of acres are flooded, which were such nice-looking crops. We've had downpours of rain, which has caused floods in a lot of areas. Rain, floods, high winds, and tornadoes lately have plagued the area. We had four trees downed the other Sunday evening. Lots of our shingles flew off from the barn roof, which needs a new one on the south side now. A barn window had also blown in, which caused a lot of glass over our bales of hay. My husband tried to pick it out of the bales as good as he could so the cows won't get it. Must've been a tornado had touched down.

Our son Albert's had a baby boy born on Albert's birthday, July 15. So they named him Albert Jr. Born at 3:07 A.M. and weighed 8 pounds, 4 ounces. This makes child number four for them. This makes me a grandmother for the twelfth time: six girls and six boys. Daughters Emma and Susan are taking turns to care for the household duties over at Albert's. Looks like I have to get in on it too, as the girls have to clean a house the next couple of days for a good friend of ours.

I also turned a year older, July 18. Daughter Emma turned a year older on July 19. Our family enjoyed a barbecued chicken and steak supper on my birthday. Of course, ice cream and cake had to be on the menu also. Son Amos's brought it and our daughter, Leah, brought a skillet casserole and Whoopie Pies (see page 154). Susan made zucchini squash bread. I will share the recipe for the bread and the casserole that Leah made.

Zucchini Squash Bread

Makes 2 loaves

3 eggs
1 cup cooking oil
2 cups sugar
2 cups peeled and grated zucchini
3 teaspoons vanilla extract
3 cups all-purpose flour
1 teaspoon salt
1 teaspoon baking soda
3 teaspoons ground cinnamon
1 teaspoon baking powder
1 cup chopped nuts

In a bowl, beat the eggs until foamy; add the oil, sugar, zucchini, and vanilla. Mix lightly, but well. Add the flour, salt, baking soda, cinnamon, and baking powder and mix. Stir in the nuts. Divide the batter into two 8½ by 5-inch greased loaf pans. Bake at 325° for 1 hour or until a toothpick inserted into the center comes out clean. Yummy!

Skillet Casserole

Serves 4 to 6

1 pound freshly ground beef
2 cups peeled and freshly grated potatoes
1 large onion, diced
1 (10¾-ounce) can condensed cream of mushroom soup
¾ cup water
12 slices American cheese

Brown the ground beef in a large skillet over medium heat. Layer the potatoes and then the onion on top of the beef. In a small bowl, stir together the soup and the water until combined. Pour the soup over the beef, potatoes, and onion. Layer the cheese slices over all. Cover the skillet and simmer over low heat for 40 minutes. The cheese will be golden and bubbly when done. Very good!

Hint: Grated carrots can also be added.

The Amish are commonly called "Pennsylvania Dutch," but this is a misnomer as we are not Dutch at all. The German word for German, **Deutsche**, sounded a lot like **Dutch** to early Americans. So the name, Pennsylvania Dutch, stuck. While there are no Amish with origins in the Netherlands, there are some with Swiss heritage. The background of the Amish in this area of Indiana is Swiss, so the German is even more out of place. My maiden name is Graber, which is a common Swiss surname.

Because of this misnaming, the word "Dutch" is still used with many Amish items today, like this omelet. The early Amish settlers made their omelets in the traditional German style. Egg Dutch is one of our favorite breakfast dishes. Each Amish family has their own slightly different variation of this dish. It's a hearty meal to appear on the table, and is easily prepared in the early morning hours, along with Hashed Brown Potatoes (see page 41) and homemade grape juice (see page 40).

Egg Dutch

5 eggs

$^1/4$ teaspoon pepper

1 cup milk

1 teaspoon salt

1 heaping tablespoon all-purpose flour

2 tablespoons margarine or butter

2 cups shredded Muenster or Colby cheese

Crumbled cooked bacon for topping

Put the eggs, pepper, milk, salt, and flour in a bowl and beat until the flour is dissolved. The mixture will have a mustard color. Melt the margarine in a skillet over low heat. Pour the mixture into the skillet and cover with a tight lid. When the omelet is cooked halfway through and the bottom is light brown, fold it in half, turn it over with a metal spatula, and finish baking. The omelet is ready when it puffs up and both sides are golden brown. Top with the cheese and bacon just before it's done cooking so the cheese has time to melt.

This is a traditional soup among the Amish, and is made by people all over. Breakfasts were simpler when I was growing up and coffee soup was on our breakfast table every morning. When Mother fixed a big bowl of coffee soup, we would take a dipper and put the coffee soup on our plates. Mother toasted the bread in the oven to give it a crispier, crunchier consistency. When we are just eating toast with butter for breakfast, we toast our bread on top of a burner on the kerosene oven. Toasting the bread inside the oven makes the bread harder, which is what you want for coffee soup.

I have always sweetened my coffee soup with cream. Some people like it sweet, but I like it not very sweet. Some of us mix cheese and potatoes in with our coffee soup. Now we mostly use crackers instead of toast, which I guess is easier than bothering to toast the bread. The soup is served in individual coffee mugs for each person. Not as many people eat coffee soup today, although some of the older folks still enjoy theirs.

Coffee Soup

Serves 4

4 cups hot coffee

4 slices bread, toasted

Sugar

Cream

Brew the coffee according to your taste. Break each slice of bread into 1-inch pieces and place in four serving bowls. Fill each bowl with steaming coffee. Add sugar and cream to your taste and stir. Serve hot.

Homemade Laundry Soap

2 cans of lye
2 quarts of soft water
5 quarts of melted grease
1/2 pound of borax

Mix lye and water in a granite dishpan or a crock. Let cool. Add the other ingredients. Stir for 10 minutes and pour into a mold.

We always have breakfast together in this family, but the mornings can be a rush with barn chores to be completed (like milking the cows, feeding the horses, and cleaning out the stables) and the menfolk preparing for the workday ahead. When I was living at home, I shared the chores with seven sisters and only one brother. The girls had to pitch in with morning chores like milking the cows, feeding the pigs, and taking care of the chickens. We had a double-deck chicken house with three thousand broilers. About eight to ten weeks after they were born they would be ready to be sold. Each morning we carried fifty-pound bags of feed up the stairs and had to feed the cows and pump the water by hand. It was hard work.

With a busy morning, a breakfast already prepared the night before can be very helpful. This recipe can be made the evening before, then kept in a cool place (like the refrigerator) overnight. In the morning it just has to be put in the oven.

Before Sunrise Omelet

Serves 6

10 slices bread, buttered on one side

1 pound chopped ham

6 eggs

3 cups milk

Lay the bread, buttered side down, in the bottom of a 9 by 13-inch baking dish. Cover the bread with the ham. In a bowl, mix together the eggs and milk. Pour the eggs over the bread and ham. Let set overnight in a cool place (refrigerator or ice chest).

In the morning, preheat the oven to 350°. Bake for 1 hour, until the eggs are golden and bubbly.

Most of the utensils I use were bought right after Ben and I were married. I like to keep all my kitchen utensils clean and in good order.

Grapes

Grapes can be used in so many ways. They make excellent juices, jellies, pies, fillings, wines, and grape butter. We use grapes that are purple in color because they are sweeter and make a better juice. The grapes are usually ripe in early autumn. We don't grow our own grapes; we buy them by the bushel from someone who is in trade to sell all kinds of fruits. We tried to grow our own grapes years ago, but failed. I think there were too many rabbits around; we gave up on growing our own grapes after that.

We usually process 200 quarts of grape juice in the autumn when the grapes are good and ripe. My daughters and I stem and wash the grapes, then we put 1 cup of grapes in a

quart jar, add $1/2$ cup of sugar (those who have sugar restrictions in their diet use less), and fill the jar with water leaving 1 inch of headspace. We put the lids and bands on the jars, then put them in a canner to process. The canner should be three-quarters full of cold water after the jars are inserted. We process the jars for 20 minutes after the boiling point.

We like to drink this grape juice for breakfast. I don't add much sugar to ours. Everyone in the family likes home-canned grape juice; in fact, at our Christmas family gathering we open the jars we processed in the fall. We never drink store-bought grape juice. Having homemade juice at family gatherings passes the tradition on. One of my granddaughters really likes home-canned grape juice since having it at our gathering.

We also process grapes into fermented grape wine for our Communion services. Communion is held twice a year, in the spring and the fall. We take the grapes from the stem and let them ferment for about a week in a loosely covered 5-gallon crock (we cover it with a board; it doesn't have to be real tight). You can use any kind of container except aluminum. Aluminum has too much acid and would not make the wine right. We take the grapes out of the crock and press them out by hand, squeezing the juice into a stainless-steel bucket. The pressed grapes are thrown out. We then put the juice into a 50-gallon wooden barrel (though some people use 15-, 20-, or 30-gallon barrels). We add 2 pounds of sugar dissolved in hot water per one gallon of grape juice. Then we pour the juice into gallon glass containers. Some people put balloons over the top of the containers. When the balloons are fully inflated, the wine is ready to use. This may take a couple of months.

Potatoes can be cooked, fried, mashed, put into casseroles, baked, added to soups, escalloped, and added to salads. We usually have our potatoes fried for breakfast, having cooked them in their jackets the evening before. Other times we peel the raw potatoes, slice them into a skillet, and fry them in lard. While most English don't use lard, we still do—it is the most flavorful fat to cook in.

I like to use red-skinned potatoes for hashed browns, and I always use salt. Some of my daughters even like catsup on their potatoes! We use a stainless-steel grater to shred the cooked potatoes, but when potatoes are uncooked they are hard so we can't put them through a shredder. We put them through a six-slot slicer instead. At one time, I just pared them by hand.

Potatoes provide a hearty beginning to the day, especially for farmers who need the energy supply for a day spent in the fields. If prepared right, these hashed browns will be crunchy outside and creamy inside.

Hashed Brown Potatoes

Serves 4

4 large red-skinned potatoes, peeled

2 tablespoons finely chopped onion

1/2 teaspoon salt

1/8 teaspoon pepper

2 tablespoons butter

2 tablespoons vegetable oil or bacon drippings

Cook the potatoes in a pot of boiling water until medium soft. Remove from the water and cool until they are easy to handle. Shred the potatoes into a bowl and toss with the onion, salt, and pepper. Heat the butter and oil in a 9- or 10-inch skillet. Pack the potato mixture firmly in the skillet, leaving a 1/2-inch space around the edge. Cook over low heat for 10 to 15 minutes, or until the bottom crust is brown. Cut the potato mixture in fourths. Turn each portion over, adding an additional 1 tablespoon of butter or oil if the potatoes stick to the skillet. Cook until brown. The edges will be crispy when done.

People often ask why Amish women wear a head covering. It is obedience to the Bible, where it says, "Every woman that prayeth or prophesieth with her head uncovered dishonoreth her head." (1 Cor. 11:5)

Before my dear husband passed away, he used to come to the breakfast table with a quarter for each grandchild. The grandkids all miss their Grandpa very much, but they still enjoy coming over for a breakfast at Grandma's. I try to have plenty of food when family comes home for a morning meal. These Cornmeal Cakes are a quick, easy, and filling recipe. The combination of ingredients will serve as a one-dish meal, and the recipe makes plenty.

Cornmeal Cakes

Makes 14 cakes

3 eggs

3 cups milk

1 teaspoon vanilla extract

1 teaspoon salt

1 tablespoon sugar

2 tablespoons melted butter

2 cups white cornmeal

2 cups all-purpose flour

1 teaspoon baking soda

2 pinches baking powder

Preserves or syrup for serving

Beat the eggs in a bowl, then add the milk and vanilla and stir. Add the salt, sugar, butter, cornmeal, flour, baking soda, and baking powder and stir for 1 minute until you have a smooth batter. Heat a griddle over medium-high heat. Sprinkle a few drops of water on the griddle. When the drops dance, the griddle is hot enough. For each cake, pour $1/2$ cup of batter on the griddle. Bake until bubbles appear on the top and the bottom is golden brown (about $2 1/2$ minutes), then flip and cook the other side, about $1 1/2$ minutes, until golden brown. Serve with preserves or syrup on top.

Some people don't like to eat the whites of an egg, but in this recipe the whole egg is eaten. I learned this recipe from our youngest daughter, Susan, who first had it for breakfast at a friend's house. I prepare this dish in a stainless-steel skillet. We used to use cast-iron skillets for cooking, but now most of us in my area have switched to stainless steel. Food looks and tastes better in them. This is an easy way to fix an egg and toast.

Egg-in-the-Nest

Serves 4

4 tablespoons margarine or butter

4 slices bread

4 eggs

Salt

Pepper

Spread margarine on both sides of each bread slice. Make a round hole in the center of each slice with the rim of a drinking glass. Place the bread slices in a skillet over medium heat. Crack an egg into each one of the holes. Toast the bread in the skillet until golden on both sides, about 5 minutes. The egg will cook while the bread is toasting. Add salt and pepper to your taste.

The Amish Cook

by Elizabeth Coblentz

February 1993

This was a nice sunshiny day but with a cold wind here at home again. I couldn't attend church services as of my back problem. Sciatica can sure be painful. Suppose some of you readers know what it can do. Is beginning to give relief if I give it plenty of rest, which is what to do with all the work around here. I'm glad the girls are here to go on ahead. What would I do without the girls, especially at such a time? With our sons being married, the girls see plenty of the barn to do the chores.

Appreciated our visitors this afternoon, including my Aunt Mary, who will be eighty-two years old, and her son Dan and wife. Also, my sister Lovina and husband and their daughter Liz, her husband, Jake, and children. Some of our married children and friends were here for supper.

When I think of what a tragedy could've struck our family on Friday afternoon: Son Amos's went home from here after assisting us with our butchering of pork and beef. He thought he could get some manure hauled yet after he came home. Well, somehow on the cart pulling the manure spreader by his horses, the seat of the cart broke off, throwing him back in front of the spreader. He yelled at the horses to stop and luckily they did stop. So I feel someone was looking over him. That's life! We never know what is in store for us, do we? Good thing we don't know what the future holds.

Daughter Liz and her husband, Levi, were here for supper tonight. Always good to see the children come home. My nephew's wife (Rose Marie) is in the hospital with a blood clot. They just had a newborn a couple of weeks ago. That made number nine for them. At last reports she remains on the serious list.

How would you like the scrambled egg recipe I made for breakfast?

Scrambled Eggs

Serves 4

1/2 pound bulk sausage, crumbled
6 eggs, beaten
1/2 cup grated sharp Cheddar cheese
1/4 teaspoon diced hot peppers
Salt
Pepper

Cook the sausage in a 10-inch skillet over medium heat until done, about 10 minutes. Remove the sausage from the pan, reserving the drippings, and set aside to drain. Add the eggs to the skillet and cook in the sausage drippings for 1 to 2 minutes. Return the sausage to the skillet and add the cheese and peppers. Cook for 1 to 2 minutes more. Turn the eggs with a spatula. Add salt and pepper to your taste. Cook for 1 more minute, until the cheese is melted and the eggs are done to your taste.

Creamed eggs are just one of the many ways we eat eggs in the morning. When Ben and I were first married we had three hens. We got three eggs a day for quite some time, which was often more than we could use. To have the chickens penned in all the time cost plenty of feed and it took a lot to care for them. When they ran loose they would get in my garden—and everywhere, it seemed—so we have bought our eggs for thirty years now.

I don't like store-bought eggs as well as I like farm eggs. It's hard to explain the difference, but farm eggs just taste fresher, and their inside color seems brighter. Since getting rid of the hens, we've bought our eggs from a local hen house a mile or two away. Farm eggs are good for baking and frying, and hard-boiled eggs are always good for salads. For this recipe, you can boil and peel the eggs the night before, then store them in a cool place (for those who have an electric refrigerator, store there). The sauce can easily be made next morning and served over hot toast.

Creamed Eggs

Serves 4 to 6

6 eggs

6 tablespoons butter

6 tablespoons all-purpose flour

1 1/2 teaspoons salt

Pinch of pepper

3 cups milk

Bread, toasted, for serving

Place the eggs in a kettle with water to cover over medium-high heat. Heat until boiling, and then boil for 5 minutes more. Remove from the heat and allow the eggs to cool. Peel the eggs and set them aside. Melt the butter in a heavy saucepan. Add the flour, salt, and pepper. Stir until well blended. Slowly add the milk, stirring constantly. Cook until smooth. Pour the sauce into a casserole dish for serving. Chop the hard-boiled eggs and stir them into the sauce. Serve on hot toast.

The following announcement, written by Elizabeth, appeared in *The Budget*, an Amish newspaper.

October 21, 1957: Nice and cool weather. Lots of flu and colds are around. Different schools are closed on account of the flu. Thursday, October 17, was the wedding day of Ben A. Coblentz and Elizabeth Graber (the writer). They were married by Bishop Mose M. Miller from Indiana.

Ben liked his griddlecakes, so we made them more often when he was with us. When I was young and still living at home, we made griddlecakes for supper. We hardly ever made them for breakfast. Mother's griddlecakes were thin. Thicker griddlecakes have more flour and eggs, which we just didn't have a lot of back then.

We make our own simple syrup out of brown sugar and water. The homemade syrup tastes sweeter than store-bought and is not as thick. It's more like a juice. We used to make it a lot more, but buying the syrup in stores is more convenient nowadays. These traditional griddlecakes can be prepared in a hurry when there's a busy workday ahead. The taste of buckwheat is on the strong side.

Griddlecakes

Makes 16 (4-inch-round) pancakes

2 cups buckwheat flour

2 eggs, beaten

2 teaspoons sugar

2 teaspoons baking powder

$^1/_8$ teaspoon salt

1$^1/_2$ cups milk

$^1/_2$ cup water

Mix the flour, eggs, sugar, baking powder, salt, milk, and water in a bowl until smooth. The batter will be thick. Heat a lightly greased griddle over medium-high heat. Sprinkle a few drops of water on the griddle. When the drops dance, the griddle is hot enough. Pour the batter onto the griddle by the cookspoonful and spread into 4-inch-wide circles. Cook until golden on one side, about 1 minute, and then flip and cook until golden on the other side, about 30 seconds.

Hint: The batter can be poured onto the griddle in quarter-cup increments if preferred; however, I've found using a large cookspoon works better because of the nice way the batter swirls around the spoon.

The Amish Cook

by Elizabeth Coblentz

May 1993

We are grandparents for the fifteenth time now. Daughter Liz and her husband, Levi, had a baby girl, born Monday morning at 7:48 A.M., weighing six pounds and thirteen ounces. This is their first child and guess what, it was named Elizabeth. So Grandma feels proud of that! So the sewing machine has been in gear to sew clothes for the sweet little bundle.

Daughter Susan took over household duties there this week now. Daughter Emma will trade off with Susan to help along, as Emma cleans houses for other people so she's unable to help all week. We are always glad to help out our children when in time of need. So right now, nobody here to help me with the household duties during the day, although the girls really help in the mornings and evenings when not on their daily job.

We had three granddaughters within three weeks. Son Amos's had a set of twin girls named Arlene and Marlene. So she must be a busy mother with five girls and one boy to care for. One good thing when they're all healthy.

Well, I've got nine caps cut out to sew. It's a covering the women and girls wear on their heads, for you readers who don't know what I mean about sewing a cap. For this area, it's to be black in color. Some areas wear the white covering. Then there's a scrap sheet I must complete, which was given to me to do for a neighbor lady who has been very sick. For a shut-in, it's a pastime to see who all got in on it. Someone buys a scrapbook and passes out the sheets to friends and relatives. The people give the sheets back to the buyer to give the completed book to the sick person or shut-in. So it's interesting to read all the different types of sheets with cards, verses, sayings, etc., on it, when a shut-in gets the book.

The rain has finally come today. It was beginning to be awfully dry. This will really boost up the garden stuff and crops also. Should make the hay fields grow.

This recipe makes for a good, filling sandwich. It may be good on a Saturday afternoon before taking a nap. Ha!

Snoozer Sandwiches

Makes 4 to 6 hearty sandwiches

1 cup ketchup
1/2 cup water
1/2 teaspoon yellow prepared mustard
2 tablespoons apple cider vinegar
1 to 1 1/2 pounds ground or finely
*   chopped ham*
1/3 cup firmly packed brown sugar
Rolls or sandwich bread for serving

Preheat the oven to 250°. Stir together the ketchup, water, mustard, vinegar, ham, and brown sugar. Spoon generous amounts of the spread between a roll or two pieces of bread and wrap each sandwich in foil. Bake for 1 hour, until the bread is toasted golden and the spread is firm and bubbly.

We used to cure our own bacon for this dish. Bacon is the side meat of a hog. As with ham and sausage, the men do the cutting of bacon on butchering day. Before slicing, we put the side meat on a table in the basement. Some people make their own sugar cure, while others buy it from the store. We wrap the side meat in brown paper sacks for several days. Then it is ready to be cut into strips with a butcher knife. I like to slice my bacon real thin, although some prefer thicker bacon.

One hog—depending on the size— could give us 10 to 20 pounds of bacon. Our hogs weighed 400 to 500 pounds, and sometimes as much as 600 pounds. When Ben and I kept pigs at home we fed them grain or slop, but we just hardly ever had any hogs. Ben thought they were messy. We had hogs at home when I was growing up, and my grown sons, Amos and Albert, both have hogs that they raise for butchering.

We use a lot of bacon during the year, for frying, to have with fried eggs and potatoes, or just in a Bacon, Lettuce, and Tomato Sandwich (see page 58). This recipe, served over Breakfast Biscuits (see page 31), is a good dish to start off the day. The eggs can be cooked, peeled, and diced the evening before and stored in a cool place, such as a refrigerator. We use ice chests to keep everything cool.*

Bacon and Egg Bake

Serves 4 to 6

6 slices bacon

$1/2$ onion, chopped

1 ($10^3/4$-ounce) can condensed cream of mushroom soup

$1/4$ cup milk

2 cups grated Colby cheese

5 hard-boiled eggs, diced

Salt

Pepper

Preheat the oven to 350°. Fry the bacon in a skillet over medium heat until crisp. Remove the bacon from the skillet and set aside. Drain the fat from the skillet, reserving 2 tablespoons. Fry the onion in the bacon fat. Stir in the soup, milk, cheese, eggs, and salt and pepper to your taste. Pour into a baking dish and top with crumbled bacon. Bake for 20 minutes until golden. Serve over Breakfast Biscuits (see page 31).

Rhubarb grows well in Indiana and in any temperate climate. It does best with lots of water, and does not grow very well where it is dry. My mother always canned her rhubarb for use in shortcakes, pies, and coffeecakes. I don't like to can mine because canning makes it so tart. I have frozen rhubarb before, but you have to use it immediately when you take it out of the freezer, otherwise it will get soggy.

During spring and summer, when the rhubarb is fresh from the garden, this rhubarb coffeecake is a favorite treat in my household. It goes well with a cup of coffee in the morning for breakfast.

Rhubarb Coffeecake

Makes 1 (9-inch) square cake

$1/2$ cup shortening

$1 1/4$ cups plus $1/3$ cup firmly packed brown sugar

2 eggs

1 teaspoon vanilla extract

$1/2$ cup milk

$1 1/2$ teaspoons lemon juice or apple cider vinegar

2 cups all-purpose flour

1 teaspoon baking soda

1 teaspoon salt

$2 1/2$ cups finely chopped fresh rhubarb

2 teaspoons ground cinnamon

1 teaspoon melted butter

Preheat the oven to 375°. Cream the shortening, $1 1/4$ cups of the brown sugar, the eggs, and vanilla in a bowl. In a separate bowl, combine the milk and lemon juice. Add this to the sugar mixture and stir well. Add the flour, baking soda, and salt, and stir until the flour is moistened. Mix in the rhubarb. Pour the batter into a greased 9-inch-square pan. In a separate bowl, mix together the remaining $1/3$ cup brown sugar, the cinnamon, and the butter and sprinkle over the top of the batter. Bake for 35 to 40 minutes, until golden brown in color. Serve warm or cold.

The Workday

Workdays are long and rigorous for Amish men. Most rise at 4:00 A.M. to milk the cows, feed the horses, and bring in the firewood. Fifty years ago, the majority of Amish men were farmers. They spent their days from dawn to dusk planting and plowing. The Amish have been able to live in agrarian isolation for almost three centuries, since settling in the United States. The self-sufficiency of the farm has allowed the Amish culture to flour-ish untouched by technology and time. Gradually, as the price of land has crept upward, the profitability of crops has drifted downward and a scarcity of land has developed. Farming has become a less viable liv-ing for many Amish men.

Most Amish, if they had their choice, would still farm, but it sim-ply isn't possible. This sociological shift has forced many Amish men to work in factories, in carpentry, and other non-Amish occupations. Even some women have begun working, opening up craft and quilt stores to serve the lucrative tourist trades. The Amish work ethic is legendary, and there are no prohibi-tions against earning money. In fact, there are even some Amish millionaires who own high-priced land or success-ful furniture businesses. Some Amish continue to work as blacksmiths, bakers, millers, and storekeepers—crafts

their families have practiced for generations. Men in these trades have been able to cling to the ways of bygone days, remaining largely untouched by technology.

Ben, in many ways, typified this new trend toward nonfarming. He spent over fifty years working as a car-penter and builder. His two sons followed him into the trade. Ben would leave home around 6:00 A.M. and often not return until dusk. His carpenter crew consisted of four or five Amish men, plus a non-Amish man. The non-Amish man would serve as the driver of the van that carried them from job to job. Days would be spent putting up roofs or sometimes con-structing whole structures. The car-penter crew became quite close-knit and associated mainly with one another. This is the type of techno-logical compromise the Amish are increasingly accustomed to. Those who spend the day working in facto-ries have to contend with electric lights and automation—things they tolerate for their paycheck but abandon when they get home. Although Ben's world included some touches of modernity during the day, once he returned home at night he sunk into a very tra-ditional Amish existence. It's becoming an increasingly dual world for Amish menfolk.

CHAPTER 2

Dinner

Although many people interchange the terms dinner and supper, to the Amish, there are clear meanings for each word. Dinner is the meal served at noon, and supper is the larger, sometimes fancier evening affair. The term lunch is rarely heard in Amish homes.

The noon meal is a breather, a break in the day that allows busy workers to rest before an afternoon's worth of work. Most Amish are early risers, beginning their day at 4:00 A.M.; therefore, a hearty noon meal, called **dinner** by most Pennsylvania German, is a must. Whether it's packed in a pail or served at home, the noon meal supplies the energy that is needed to make it through the rest of the day. It's a lighter meal than supper, as too much food can make one drowsy during the afternoon, but this doesn't mean the meal isn't filling and sometimes even elegant.

Often the girls and I will come in from working in the garden for the whole morning to have a quick dinner. We'll put together some sandwiches, laying out sliced tomatoes, lettuce, sliced cheese, and maybe even some Smoked Summer Sausage (see page 72). Summer sausage is such a quick and handy meat to have on hand for sandwiches. Children take their dinner to school in a bucket, while menfolk farmers come back to the house for their break. It is always a chore to decide what to pack in those dinner buckets, but a Homemade Ham Salad Spread (see page 56) or a Garden Sandwich Spread (see page 55) are often included. Noon dinners served after weddings or as a break during a barn-raising day are full-course meals with everything that would normally be served during a big supper. On these days, the evening supper is usually a lighter meal of leftovers.

The Amish Cook

by Elizabeth Coblentz

September 1993

Daughters Emma, Susan, Liz, and I went to my daughter Leah's to help her prepare dinner for a total of seventy-six children. The dinner was to be taken to their one-room Amish school where their two children attend.

The menu consisted of mashed potatoes, beef and gravy, corn, macaroni and cheese, sliced tomatoes, lettuce salad, sweet pepper strips, dip and crackers, pretzel sticks, watermelons, three kinds of cakes, two kinds of cookies, three kinds of pop, and bread. It was a question on her to see how much she should prepare for all, as to not run out. But she had more than plenty for all, for which Leah was glad.

When the food was ready by 10:00 A.M., we loaded up the food, plus the paper plates, foam cups, silverware, and lots of other cooking utensils onto a two-seated horse and buggy and headed for the school, which was a six-mile drive. It takes longer by buggy than by a car, so we left by 10:30 A.M., taking in an enjoyable ride, and the weather was ideal. How relaxing, after all the morning rush.

We arrived at the school and got unloaded and headed for the basement with the food. The students were wondering who was bringing dinner, as the teacher told them no lunch boxes had to be brought that day. She kept it a secret, though, as to why the kids didn't have

to pack a lunch. Everyone was looking forward to it. Every once in a while, some parents bring dinner in to the school, which is quite a treat for all.

We were ready to eat by 11:30 A.M. and, after everyone had eaten, we cleared the tables and packed up to go back to daughter Leah's. But we visited the classroom awhile before heading back, which was quite interesting. It was great to see all those little students thanking Leah for dinner. After we got back to Leah's, we washed all the dirty dishes, stainless-steel canners and kettles, and put the leftover food in smaller containers. There seemed to be plenty left.

It was such a relaxing, enjoyable day, working together, preparing food, and driving together on the two-seated buggy. The air seemed so fresh.

It was also a day planned to clean my mother's house, but Leah had the school meal planned first and I had promised her we'd help her as it would have been too much for her to do this all by herself, preparing all the food and taking it there. So Susan and I will help mother tomorrow clean her house, as I know it wasn't all cleaned today.

Daughter Liz and family returned home Sunday morning from the Smoky Mountains. They had van trouble, so didn't make it home on time (Amish people are allowed to own only horse and buggies for travel, but can occasionally be transported in a van by a non-Amish driver).

Well I am getting sleepy so I must hike to happy landing. Daughter Liz and family just

left as they were here for supper. I hope all you readers out there are in good health. I will share some recipes for treats we took to the school. Kids think they are yummy!

Applesauce Cookies

Makes 3 dozen cookies

2 cups all-purpose flour
1 teaspoon baking soda
1/4 teaspoon salt
1 teaspoon ground cinnamon
1/2 teaspoon ground nutmeg
1/2 cup butter
1/2 cup sugar
1/2 cup firmly packed brown sugar
1 egg
1 cup Applesauce (see page 93)
1 cup old-fashioned oatmeal
1/2 cup raisins (optional)
1/2 cup nuts (optional)
1/2 cup chocolate chips

Preheat the oven to 375°. In a bowl, sift together the flour, baking soda, salt, cinnamon, and nutmeg. Set aside. In another bowl, mix together the butter, sugars, and egg. Add the applesauce, oatmeal, raisins, nuts, and chocolate chips. Add the sifted ingredients and mix real well, until the batter is smooth. Drop by teaspoonfuls, spaced apart, onto cookie sheets. Bake for 10 minutes, until the top and edges are slightly brown. Allow the cookies to cool for 5 minutes before removing to wire racks to cool completely.

Buttermilk Brownies

Makes about 15 (3-inch) brownies

2 cups sugar
2 cups all-purpose flour
1/4 teaspoon salt
4 tablespoons unsweetened
    cocoa powder
1 cup cold water
1/2 cup butter
1/2 cup vegetable oil
1/2 cup buttermilk
1 teaspoon baking soda
2 eggs
1/2 teaspoon vanilla extract

Preheat the oven to 400°. Sift the sugar, flour, salt, and cocoa together in a bowl. In a saucepan, bring the water, butter, and oil to a boil. Pour over the sugar mixture and beat until creamy. Add the buttermilk, baking soda, eggs, and vanilla. Stir thoroughly. The batter will be thin and soupy. Pour into a greased 9 by 13-inch baking pan. Bake for 30 minutes, until the sides begin to pull away from the pan and a toothpick inserted into the center comes out clean.

Garden Sandwich Spread

Makes 12 cups

When I was a little girl attending a country school, I always took my dinner in a pail for the noon meal. The school had one room with a "big" side and a "little" side. First, second, third, and fourth grades were on one side, and fifth, sixth, seventh, and eighth grades were on the other. There was a movable wall that separated the sides, and sometimes the teachers would open the wall to bring the sides together. I think there were only four students on my side.

Times were tight then, so sometimes dinner would just be a mustard sandwich. Times are better today, so this sandwich spread has more ingredients in it, giving it a richer taste. Some people enjoy eating it alone on a sandwich, and some people spread it on cuts of ham and turkey in place of mayonnaise or mustard.

12 green tomatoes

12 green mangoes, peeled and pitted

12 red mangoes, peeled and pitted

1 large onion, finely chopped

1 cup yellow prepared mustard

1/2 cup sugar

1/4 cup salt

1 tablespoon celery seed

4 cups Salad Dressing (see page 167) or Miracle Whip

Coarsely chop the tomatoes and mangoes and put through a hand-grinder (or pulse in an electric food processor) until medium ground. Place in a 12 1/2-quart kettle with the onion, mustard, sugar, salt, and celery seed. Stir together until yellow in color and smooth. Boil for 15 minutes over medium heat. Remove the kettle from the stove, add the salad dressing, and mix well. The mixture will turn a lighter yellow color. Put the kettle back on the stove over a real low heat while filling clean, sterilized jars with the spread. Seal while hot.

Hint: I use a "Victoria strainer" (see photo page 72) to grind the tomatoes and mangoes. It's a hand-cranked machine that reduces the fruit to the size of peas or raisins and leaves plenty of juice.

Thinking back to my lower school years, I have many memories of my one-room country school. One of the good memories is of recess. We enjoyed playing ball and games like hide-and-go-seek, hopscotch, and jump rope. When the weather was nasty outside, we played Red Rover and board games like checkers and marbles in the basement. If we wanted a drink, we had to pump our own water from the pump outside the door. It was always fresh water. Our children today don't know what it was like to go out in all kinds of weather to pump water at school. All eight of our children attended the public schools, and they have modern, indoor plumbing. Often I think about how we'd run for those outhouses (one for girls and one for boys) in cold, snowy weather. We didn't complain because we were used to it being this way in our country school.

Our dinner pails were put on shelves in a small room, near where our coats, bonnets, and caps were hung. This is a good recipe for dinner buckets or dinner pails. I often fixed it for my children when they went to school. When I was a child, ham was more expensive, so bologna or wiener sandwiches were made instead. This tasty sandwich will stay nice and fresh until the noon hour.

Homemade Ham Salad Spread

Serves 4 to 6; makes about 2 1/2 cups

1 pound cooked ham, coarsely chopped

3 small stalks celery, finely diced

1 large dill pickle, finely diced

1 1/4 teaspoons dry mustard

1/4 teaspoon onion powder

1/2 cup Homemade Mayonnaise (see page 167) or store-bought mayonnaise

1/2 teaspoon salt

1 tablespoon lemon juice

Put the cooked ham through a hand-grinder (or pulse in an electric food processor) until medium ground. Mix together the ham, celery, and pickle in a bowl. In a separate bowl, combine the mustard, onion powder, mayonnaise, salt, and lemon juice and stir. (Additional mayonnaise may be added to suit your taste.) Stir this mixture into the ham. Spread onto sandwich bread to serve.

Hint: This ham salad tastes even better the next day after being refrigerated overnight. It also tastes great on crackers.

Dinner Buckets

In the morning, dinner buckets are packed with whatever food is on hand. There might be seven, eight, or even more buckets to pack in a big family like ours. We pack some buckets for school, and some for those who work away from home as carpenters or in factories during the day. At the end of a week, there are lots of groceries to be bought at the store for the next week's dinners.

The children nowadays would probably turn up their noses at what was in our dinner buckets when we were small. When I was a little girl, Mother would pack a jar of milk, homemade apple-butter sandwiches, a home-baked cookie, and apples or tomatoes, depending on what was in season. Sometimes Mother would make Poor Man's Bread Pie (see page 71) for the dinner buckets, which was bread, milk, flour, sugar, and cinnamon baked in a pie shell. A slice of bread pie was always a great treat. We also had grapes from our grapevines, yellow mustard sandwiches, and once in awhile, bologna sandwiches, which we thought were great.

I reckon we were more satisfied back then than children are today. Today there are "better" sandwiches, prepackaged potato chips, pretzels, all kinds of baked goodies, and candy bars—mostly store-bought stuff. Back then we didn't think to say, "I don't like this" or "I don't like that." The dinner buckets were packed and we were thankful to open them and eat what was inside. We lived to be strong and healthy with a simple noon meal out of our dinner buckets at school.

The hours seem to melt away when we go out to the garden to hoe in the morning. Before you know it, several hours have slipped by, the sun is shining brightly, and it is dinnertime. With a bountiful garden, there are plenty of options: lettuce, radishes, green onions, tomatoes, carrots, and cucumbers could all be on the menu. The green onions are cleaned, the tomatoes are washed and sliced, radishes and carrots are pulled from the ground, and the cucumbers are washed, peeled, and sliced.

Bacon, tomatoes, lettuce, ham, and cheese make for good dinner sandwiches. We also fix some more unusual, but tasty, sandwiches from the garden: radishes with margarine on bread, sweet peppers with margarine, or onion and mustard sandwiches, which were common when I was growing up. This delicious bacon, lettuce, and tomato sandwich is best with vegetables right from the garden.

Bacon, Lettuce, and Tomato Sandwich   Serves 4

8 slices bacon

8 slices Homemade Bread (see page 80) or store-bought white bread

8 slices tomatoes

8 slices Colby or Swiss cheese

8 leaves oak leaf or iceberg lettuce

4 teaspoons Salad Dressing (see page 167) or Miracle Whip

Fry the bacon in a skillet over medium heat until crisp, about 5 minutes. Take the bacon from the skillet and set aside to drain. Take 1 slice of bread and layer with 2 slices of tomato, 2 slices of bacon, 2 slices of cheese, and 2 leaves of lettuce. Spread 1 teaspoon of the salad dressing on a second slice of bread and place facedown on top of the lettuce to complete the sandwich. Repeat for each sandwich.

The Amish Cook

by Elizabeth Coblentz

August 1994

A procession of black buggies is moving through the morning mist. They are on their way to Sunday services, a pleasant morning for a ride in the fresh, fall-like air. Our church district has services every other Sunday; this is our week to stay home. These buggies belong to another district. The people in the buggies are wearing their Sunday best, which we always try to do when going to services. Men in our district aren't allowed to have buttons on their jackets, vests, and shirts, only "hooks and eyes." The women wear dark blue dresses and black bonnets.

We will spend this morning at home, resting. Ben is reading *The Budget,* an Amish newspaper, and the daughters have scattered through the house, each doing their own thing. Except for youngest, Susan, and Emma, who are working together on some needlepoint.

This afternoon will be spent doing some of the things necessary to prepare for the long, hard winter ahead. Ben and son-in-law Joe will chop wood, as to have plenty for the cookstoves. It is never too early to begin preparing. The daughters and I will work on canning, for which the garden has provided us plenty. It is so nice in the cold of winter to open up the jars and smell the sweet scents of summer. Lots of work, though, to can.

Yesterday was also spent doing chores to prepare for winter. Next week Ben will check the chimneys. Hard to believe the first frost is now probably only six weeks away. The girls weeded and hoed the garden. They saved the weeds and fed them to our bull, which is a useful way to get rid of them.

When going out to the clothesline this morning, I wasn't wearing any shoes, and on the dew-wet grass, I slipped. I slid right into the pole. I was okay, but my ankle is a little sore. Ben says I should try out for a baseball team, because I slid so well.

Ha!

My aged mother will spend a few days with us next week. I am going to sew her a dress, and the girls are fixing up a room in the house. Hard to believe she will be ninety next year. We try to see to it that she gets good care when she stays with us. Those long days can be lonely when you are ninety.

It will be a rushy Monday, spending time preparing the place for her visit, and the canning time will be in full gear. Daughter Liz is coming over later this afternoon, so Susan will get some cookies going for the grandkids. Here is the cookie recipe she will fix.

Chewy Oatmeal Cookies

Makes about 5 dozen cookies

1 cup sugar
1 cup firmly packed brown sugar
1 cup lard or shortening
2 eggs
1 teaspoon vanilla extract
3 cups old-fashioned oatmeal
2 cups sifted all-purpose flour
1/2 teaspoon salt
1 teaspoon baking soda

Preheat the oven to 350°. In a bowl, cream the sugars thoroughly with the lard until the mixture is light and fluffy and no granules remain. Beat in the eggs until light. Add the vanilla and stir. Stir in the oatmeal. In a separate bowl, mix together the flour, salt, and baking soda. Work the dry ingredients into the oatmeal mixture. Drop by teaspoonfuls, spaced apart, onto cookie sheets. Bake for 10 to 12 minutes, until the center is soft to the touch and the top and edges are golden to light brown in color. Allow the cookies to cool for 5 minutes before removing to wire racks to cool completely.

This soup is always easy to prepare as it is one of many meals that can be fixed without a trip to the store. A lot of the readers of my weekly newspaper column don't think we ever go to the grocery store, but Amish people are just like everybody else in some ways. We don't need to buy some things, like vegetables during the summer when we have our garden, but during the winter we buy carrots if we run out. And Jell-O and crackers are items we can't make so we buy them at the store.

I like this soup because the potatoes, noodles, beef, and onion are all cooked in one kettle, which makes for less washing of dishes. Without an electric dishwasher, having fewer dishes to wash comes in handy! You can also use spaghetti in this soup instead of the homemade noodles. We use canned beef from our slaughtered steer, and usually a supply of homemade noodles and homegrown potatoes and onions.

One-Kettle Soup

Serves 4 to 6

1 quart home-canned chunk beef, or
1 pound store-bought stew beef, cubed

4 potatoes, peeled and diced

6 ounces dried Amish Noodles (see page 87) or thin, store-bought noodles

1 onion, chopped

Salt

Pepper

Fill a 6-quart kettle with 3 quarts of water and bring to a hard boil over high heat. Reduce the heat to low and add the beef. Simmer until tender, about 2 hours. Remove the beef and set aside, reserving the water in the kettle. Add enough water to the kettle water to measure a total of 3 quarts. Add the potatoes, noodles, and onion to the kettle and return the water to a hard boil over high heat. Cook for about 8 minutes, until the vegetables and noodles are soft. Return the beef to the kettle and continue boiling for 12 minutes more. Add salt and pepper to your taste and serve.

Hint: Do not overcook or too much liquid will be lost.

The are "winter" soups and there are "summer" soups. On a cold winter's night when the snow is swirling outside, certain soups taste good and warm you to the bone. On a warm summer day, there's nothing better than a light soup made with vegetables straight from the garden.

Like soups, our chores also change with the seasons. In the winter, there are ash-pans to empty from the wood and coal stoves, and firewood and several buckets of coal to be brought in each evening. We buy our coal from a local supplier who delivers it to us. During the summer, there are gardens to be planted and hoed, and lawns to be mowed. There are also plenty of flowers—geraniums, marigolds, and tulips—to be cared for. We plant marigolds throughout the garden as they keep the rabbits away. I've seen gardens surrounded by several rows of marigolds, with marigolds planted between the rows of vegetables, too.

Our meals don't change much from season to season because we have our supply of canned foods, but during the summer we have fresh fruits and vegetables from the garden. This vegetable soup tastes good any time of year.

Garden Vegetable Soup

Serves 4 to 6

2 cups tomato juice

1 quart browned home-canned chunk beef, or 1 pound browned ground beef

1 cup peeled and diced potato

1/2 cup chopped celery

1 cup diced carrot

1 onion, chopped

1 1/2 teaspoons salt

Put the tomato juice and beef in a 4-quart kettle and add the potato, celery, carrot, and onion. Season with salt. Cook over high heat just until boiling, then turn the heat to low. Cover the kettle and cook for 15 minutes longer, just until the vegetables are soft and tender. The soup should be colorful, with a tomato-colored juice.

Hint: Some people use 1 pound of ground beef in place of the chunk beef, but I think the home-canned beef has a better taste and isn't as greasy.

Here's a poem I read once but only remember part of; it captures my love of the growing season:

First comes asparagus, lettuce, and peas
Oh! How good taste all of these.
Strawberries, onions, radishes, and string beans,
Carrots, limas, and turnip greens.
Corn, potatoes, and cabbage for kraut—
Much of this we'll have this summer, no doubt.
Tomatoes, red beets and pickles, also some dill—
All of these help my garden to fill.

Author Unknown

Elizabeth's Gardening Tips

❋ To make flowers grow, soak eggshells in warm water for twenty-four hours. Remove the shells and use the water to water your flowers.

❋ Lay black plastic garbage bags around pickle and melon plants to avoid weeds and to double the yield.

❋ Plant your cabbage in onion rows. By the time the cabbage plants need more room, the onions have been pulled for eating.

❋ Plant marigolds to keep the bugs and rabbits away.

❋ Put some wood ashes on the ground where you plant radishes to keep the worms away.

❋ Dust your tomato and lettuce plants with talcum powder to keep the birds and rabbits away.

❋ Put generous handfuls of mothballs around your garden during the summer season to keep deer and other large animals away.

❋ Use lightweight plastic gallon milk jugs to protect your plants from freezing. Cut off the bottom and place over your early plants. Leave the cap off and push the jugs well into the ground to keep the wind from blowing them away.

Some people around here still make their own cheese. I often make homemade cottage cheese, but not the cheese used in this recipe. This is another good soup recipe to prepare for the noon meal, especially when you use those fresh vegetables from the garden. This soup has a good, cheesy flavor.

Velvety Cheese Soup

1/4 cup butter

1/4 cup minced onion

1/4 cup all-purpose flour

4 cups milk

Salt

1 cup grated Cheddar cheese

2 cups fresh vegetable pieces, such as corn, diced carrots, or peas

Melt the butter in a saucepan over medium-high heat. Add the onion and sauté until clear. Remove the pan from the heat. Add the flour, milk, and salt to your taste. Return the saucepan to the heat and cook until thick, stirring constantly. Add the cheese and stir until melted. Add the vegetables. Let simmer for 30 minutes over low heat and serve warm.

Hint: Frozen vegetable pieces may also be used. You don't have to cook them before you add them to the soup as they will cook in the soup.

Yes, the Amish pay taxes like anyone else. The Amish, though, feel that the church is responsible to care for its own poor, aged, and infirmed and accordingly do not accept government subsidies, welfare, or pensions.

An assortment of soups is served at an after-church meal, with a good chili soup being one of the most popular around here. Right after church services, the tables are set for the meal. We have two tables for the women and two tables for the men. The food is cooking in the kitchen during services. This way everyone is seated for the meal soon after church. The food is placed on the tables before everyone is seated, and we have a silent prayer together before eating. The older people usually eat first and when they are done, the tables are reset so more people can eat. There are usually more than a hundred people at a church service, so the tables sometimes have to be reset several times.

Potato soup, cheese soup, and onion soup are frequently served at after-church meals, but this chili soup is one we often make for our large gatherings. While many people use ground beef in their chili soup, I prefer the flavor of fresh sausage. My family seems to enjoy this recipe.

Winter's Day Chili Soup

Serves 15

1 cup chopped onion

2 pounds bulk sausage

2 quarts tomato juice, warmed

1/2 cup firmly packed brown sugar

3/4 teaspoon chili powder

1/8 teaspoon red pepper flakes (optional)

Salt

6 cups water

4 rounded tablespoons cornstarch

4 cups cooked kidney beans

In a stainless-steel skillet, sauté the onion and sausage until browned. Drain the grease and place the onion and sausage into a 6-quart kettle with the tomato juice, brown sugar, chili powder, red pepper, salt to your taste, and 4 cups of the water. Heat the kettle over medium heat until boiling. Dissolve the cornstarch in the remaining 2 cups of water. Add the cornstarch mixture to the kettle and stir until thickened. Add the beans. Cook for 5 to 10 minutes, until the beans are heated through. Serve warm.

Hint: I warm my tomato juice to just below the boiling point before adding it to the kettle. This is the way my mother always made this soup. For those who like a spicier soup, add more chili powder.

The Amish Cook

by Elizabeth Coblentz

October 1994

Today we're having our thirty-seventh wedding anniversary. Ben and I were married October 17, 1957. This morning at the breakfast table, Ben reminded me that thirty-seven years ago I was busy frying chicken, starting at 4:00 A.M. The cooks were to fry several hundred pounds of chicken for the wedding dinner.

The Asian flu struck our area a couple of weeks before our wedding. It was a severe epidemic of influenza caused by a virus strain. So many were down with that flu, including some of our family. Mother was still in bed the Tuesday before our Thursday wedding. A friend brought Mother a salve she had made, it was called a tobacco salve and it was rubbed on the chest only and right now she snapped out of it. My fever went up to 105 degrees a week before the wedding day. Having that much fever at the age of twenty-one, I still remember it. But I got back to feeling better the week of our wedding, although I was weak.

In the years since our wedding, we have been blessed with six daughters and two sons. We still have three daughters at home. The rest are married and have families of their own. We have seventeen grandchildren, which there's ten girls and seven boys. Six of the grandchildren are in school now. Time has a way of slipping by. We're always glad to see them come. We can always pour more water to the soup. So I'll put pork, steak, and chicken on the grill tonight in case someone from our family shows up for the evening meal. The menu has been planned.

Still some garden goodies out there. We still have tomatoes, but the frost got a hold of some. We have nice prize-head lettuce, also hot and sweet peppers, turnips, carrots, endive, onions, a couple types of cabbages, red beets, winter radishes, and sweet potatoes. But this time of year we'll have to get some out of the ground before a good freeze comes. It is remarkable how things have done so well in this dry weather. Very dry!

Daughter Verena and I dug out the *Canna* bulbs on Saturday evening and put other various bulbs in the ground. The trees are losing their beautiful leaves of red, yellow, and orange. Looking at the woods, the leaves are in their autumn splendor. What a beautiful scene.

A year ago, we were preparing for the forthcoming reunion of my mother's family, with a good turnout. We also had our first snow of the season. Mother is still living, but we have lost a brother-in-law.

Well, the huge wash out on the clothesline seems to be drying well with this autumn breeze. The temperature is 82 degrees. I have more to hang out as we had too much for the lines to hold. Daughter Lovina and I did our wash together in our wash house with our motorless washer. It's what you call an arm strong. Ha!

Well enough for this time. Happy thirty-seventh anniversary for us! Will share a recipe that will help to use some garden goodies.

Fresh Vegetable Pizza

Serves 4 to 6

1 uncooked Homemade Pizza Dough (see page 169) or 2 (8-ounce) packages refrigerated crescent rolls
2 (8-ounce) packages cream cheese, softened
1 cup Homemade Mayonnaise (see page 167) or store-bought mayonnaise
1 (16-ounce) package dried ranch salad dressing mix
1/2 cup chopped onion
1/2 cup chopped cauliflower
1/2 cup chopped broccoli
1/2 cup chopped radish
1/2 cup chopped celery
1/2 cup chopped green bell pepper
1/2 cup chopped carrot
1/2 cup chopped tomato (optional)
8 ounces Cheddar cheese, grated

Preheat the oven to 350°. Roll out the dough as directed on page 147 and line a 10 1/2 by 15 1/2-inch jelly-roll pan. If using packaged crescent rolls, unroll, but do not separate the rolls, and press them into the jelly-roll pan. Bake for 10 minutes, until the dough is golden brown. Set aside to cool. Mix the cream cheese, mayonnaise, and salad dressing mix in a bowl and spread over the cooled crust. Top with the vegetables and sprinkle the Cheddar cheese over all. Cut into 12 or 24 squares and refrigerate until ready to serve.

A large selection of salads is served at our after-church dinner. Such salads might include a carrot salad, a bean salad, or a Waldorf, Watergate, or Jell-O salad. Potato salad and slaw seem to be served more often in the winter, with lighter salads being served during the summer.

My family likes to eat any kind of salad. When I was in my mother's care we didn't have all kinds of salads, as they were considered a fancier food during those tight times. Lettuce was on the menu when it was in season, cabbage was raised from the garden and stored for the winter, and we ate sliced cucumbers in sour cream when they were in season. Sometimes Mother would add diced onions to the cucumbers and sour cream.

Nowadays we eat more salads. This seven-layer salad is a favorite one to fix as it uses so much from the garden. We often serve it for the after-church meal.

Simple Seven-Layer Salad

Serves 6

1 head iceberg or 2 heads Bibb lettuce

2 cups fresh or frozen peas or cauliflower pieces

1 onion, thinly sliced

4 hard-boiled eggs, chopped

$^1/_2$ cup chopped celery

1 pound bacon, fried and coarsely chopped

2 cups Homemade Mayonnaise (see page 167) or store-bought mayonnaise

$^1/_3$ cup sugar

2 cups grated Cheddar cheese

Crumbled cooked bacon for garnish (optional)

Chop or tear the lettuce into 1-inch pieces. Spread the lettuce over the bottom of a 2-quart casserole dish. Then layer the peas, onion, egg, celery, and bacon. In a separate bowl, combine the mayonnaise and sugar until thin and smooth. Spread on top of the salad to make the seventh layer. Do not stir. Chill for 12 hours. Before serving, sprinkle with the cheese and bacon.

Church Dinners

In Amish communities, churches are divided into districts. There are twenty to thirty families in a church, making a total of one hundred fifty to two hundred or more persons to a district. When a district's size increases too much, it is divided.

Each district has four ministers: a bishop, a deacon, and two ministers. The bishop is the leader of each church district and determines the Ordnung. The Ordnung is an unwritten but faithfully followed set of rules that every church member follows in daily life. Some rules vary from district to district because different bishops have different rules.

Sunday church services and church dinners are held in our homes. Church is held every other week so people have a chance to visit other communities on some Sundays. Church begins at 9:00 A.M. and lets out toward noon. Benches are set up in the home to accommodate all the people in attendance for the service and the after-church meal. The benches are stored in a bench wagon, which is pulled from home to home each week.

In the morning, before the service begins, cookies and crackers are passed around for the smaller children. Sometimes pretzels or candy are also served. It's such a delight for the young children. The single girls help prepare for dinner, putting the jams, jellies, red beets, and pickles onto dishes to be set out for the meal. There is bologna, ham, cheese, store-bought and home-baked bread, hot peppers, and hot pepper butter. A favorite at after-church meals in Indiana Amish communities is a peanut butter mixture, made from a light corn syrup, peanut butter, and marshmallow cream. We use the amount of each that we prefer, and many people make a sandwich out of the spread.

In season, there are tomatoes, lettuce, radishes, and sweet and hot peppers from the garden. These vegetables vary from place to place, depending on our neighbors' gardens. I always like to see a variety of food on everyone's table for a Sunday dinner. Some kind of soup, which is served with crackers, is always made for the smaller children and babies.

The single girls and hosting family members watch the tables to see that the dishes stay filled. Tables are set up for the men and boys, and for the women and girls. Men and women eat separately at the noon dinner. After the meal, the women and girls pitch in to wash all those dishes.

In our church, most of the women also invite everyone to come back for the evening meal. It's usually a cooked meal with lots of desserts, baked goods, and salads. Visiting takes place after the noon meal, which always seems enjoyable after services. We talk about the latest happenings among the members of our church. Occasionally, some Amish strangers from faraway churches come to a service, usually visiting family in the area. A lot of times we don't see each other until the next church service, so there is a lot to catch up on.

Choosing the lettuce to use in a salad can be difficult for someone just starting out, but through the years I have learned what kinds work best. I grow several varieties of lettuce, including iceberg, prizehead, buttercrunch, and oak leaf. Prizehead and oak leaf last better in the Indiana heat. The buttercrunch, which we plant earlier in the spring, has a sweet taste and grows into heads, but the oak leaf and iceberg just grow as leaves. I don't like the iceberg as well as I like the other three; it has more of a green taste.

For this salad you can really use any kind of lettuce. This recipe also calls for peas, which I don't grow often. It's a lot of work to grow and pot peas, and we don't use that many peas to begin with. Be careful not to use more than 12 strips of bacon, as it has a strong taste.

Food that can be prepared the day before a large dinner is always a help as it cuts down on the work that has to be done the morning of the meal. This overnight salad has a delicious taste by the next morning.

Emma's Overnight Salad

Serves 4 to 6

1 head lettuce

1 head cauliflower

1 cup fresh or frozen peas

1 onion, diced

1 cup loosely packed shredded carrot

2 cups Salad Dressing (see page 167) or Miracle Whip

1/3 cup sugar

8 to 12 strips crisply cooked bacon, crumbled

2 cups shredded mild Cheddar cheese

Tear the lettuce into 1-inch pieces and place in a large bowl. Break the cauliflower into 1-inch pieces and add to the bowl along with the peas, onion, and carrot. In a separate bowl, stir together the salad dressing and the sugar. Spread this mixture on top of the vegetables in a thin layer, as if you were icing a cake. Sprinkle the crumbled bacon and cheese over the top. Chill overnight and serve the next day. Delicious!

Mother used to bake this pie when I was in my lower grades at school. This was a handy pie for the dinner buckets, but we would also have it for a meal sometimes. In later years, I fixed bread pie for my own family. My two sons were fond of bread pie when they were children. Amos and Albert would come in and say "Mom, do you have enough dough to make a bread pie yet?"

Some people think homemade bread pie tastes like pumpkin pie, with its creamy texture. One time, Ben thought he was eating a piece of pumpkin pie, which he enjoys, and then someone told him he was eating bread pie. He liked it until he knew what kind of pie it was! Ben never cared much for bread pie, but he kept eating that piece. This is called "poor man's" pie because of the simple ingredients in it. I like to use bread that is on the hard side. Soft bread does not crumble up as well. I crumble the bread real fine and I like a lot of cinnamon.

Poor Man's Bread Pie

Serves 4 to 6

1 (8-inch) unbaked Never-Fail Pie Crust (see page 127)

Crumbled hard bread, enough to fill pie shell

5 teaspoons sugar

1 tablespoon all-purpose flour

2 tablespoons ground cinnamon

5 to 7 cups milk

Preheat the oven to 375°. Roll out the crust and line an 8-inch pie pan, as directed on page 127. Place the bread in the pie shell till the bread comes even to the top of the crust. Add the sugar, flour, and cinnamon, sprinkling it evenly over the top of the bread. Fill the pie shell with milk to within $1/2$ inch of the top edge. Bake until the pie is firm in the middle and you don't see any juice in the center.

Many Amish carry calling cards—a personal card they leave with friends after visiting.

Summer sausage sandwiches with green onions, lettuce, and sliced tomatoes used to be popular around here. We would make our own summer sausage using home-butchered sausage, ground beef from our steer, and seasonings. I sewed muslin sacks, five inches wide and thirty inches long, which were filled with the mixture. We had to leave the sausage hanging in those sacks awhile until Ben smoked them in our smokehouse with hickory wood. In four to six weeks, after three good smokings from the hickory wood, it was ready to eat.

Smoked summer sausage makes the best sandwiches. You just have to slice off a hunk to make a hearty and delicious meal. Summer sausage is also good to eat with cheese and crackers, especially when company arrives unexpectedly and you want to serve them a quick snack. We used to make a hundred pounds of summer sausage every year. As our family grew older and the kids moved away, we made summer sausage less and less.

Smoked Summer Sausage

Makes 100 pounds

66 pounds freshly ground beef

5 pounds sugar

33 pounds ground pork

1/3 pound pepper

4 tablespoons salt

2 ounces saltpeter

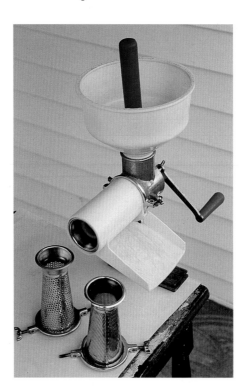

Put a clean tablecloth on a long table and put all the ingredients on the cloth. Mix as you would for sausage and stuff the mixture tightly in muslin sacks (5 inches wide by 30 inches long). Hang the sacks in a cellar for 1 to 2 weeks and then smoke three times for a minimum of 2 hours each time. Let dry in the cellar for 6 to 8 weeks. Good eating.

The Amish Cook

by Elizabeth Coblentz

Feburary 1995

As we enter a new month, February, what will this month hold? I feel this morning we had luck with the unlucky. The morning rush had such a good start. Breakfast dishes were washed before the girls left for the sewing factory at 5:30 A.M. My husband left for work at 6:00 A.M. So the rest of the morning duties were done and I started this task of writing and Susan was ironing. What a relaxing morning, but how long did it last?

After 7:00 A.M., all at once we heard such a roaring sound in the chimney. My, such a roar! I opened the Hitzer stove door to see how the fire was coming along, as being a warm winter we hadn't fired much this year. The stovepipe wasn't hot but it was black in the chimney. So I went outside to check the chimney and there was such a rolling black smoke billowing out of the top.

I ran inside and dumped three pounds of salt on the fire, but no luck. The black smoke rushing out of the chimney became worse. What a scare!

So it happened our neighbor (Sam Q.) and wife who lives north of us came along and assisted us, and he just took over. We got a ladder and he got up on top of the roof and poured three pounds of salt down the chimney. Again, no luck! So he asked if we should pour water down slowly on it, so I said, "We'll have to do something to get that chimney fire out." We went back into the house and looked up the chimney with a mirror under the fireplace and seen the fire. So he took a bucket of water and poured it down the chimney. And still no luck. So we got another bucket of water and poured it down the chimney. This done the trick! What a relief to not have a gutted-out house and maybe no house at all. We were just glad to have a house to clean up a mess in.

So in the evening when my husband came home from work, he got on top of the roof with a chain to clean the chimney out. The chain didn't seem to go through, so he got a long rod and poked it, which at once a huge pile of creosote came down. Then the chain was used to clean the rest of it out. There were at least three coal buckets or more full of creosote in the chimney. Again, a mess to clean up.

So our kitchen stove also was cleaned out. Too much creosote in a chimney can really cause a fire. Never seen such in all of thirty-eight years of marriage. So you all be careful with those chimneys.

Before the fire started, the girls ate a breakfast pizza. It is filling and keeps them nourished in the long hours until lunch. Following is the recipe, which calls for easy ingredients like frozen hashed brown potatoes, or you can make your own hashed browns (see page 41).

Breakfast Pizza

Serves 6

1 pound bulk pork sausage
1 uncooked Homemade Pizza Dough
(see page 169)
1 cup peeled and shredded potatoes
1 cup grated Cheddar cheese
2 tablespoons grated Parmesan cheese
4 eggs
3 tablespoons milk
Salt
Pepper

Preheat the oven to 375°. Brown the sausage and drain well. Set aside to cool. Roll out the dough and line a pizza pan or baking sheet as directed on page 147. Spoon the cooled sausage over the crust. Sprinkle the potato and the cheeses over the top. In a bowl, beat together the eggs, milk, and a dash each of salt and pepper. Pour over the potatoes and cheese. Bake for 30 minutes, until the top turns golden brown.

CHAPTER 3

Supper

Supper is the time for everyone to gather together after a hard day's work, enjoy each other's company, and have a big, hearty meal. During wintertime, darkness falls early in northern Indiana, so supper is enjoyed by the glow of a warm kerosene lamp. The meal is made more special by everyone bowing their heads in silent prayer before feasting.

Suppers weren't always so fancy, though. When I was still living at home, margarine was saved for Sundays and butter was used the rest of the week. Margarine was considered special. Mother tried to save money whenever she could. On the next road over there was a patch of wild strawberries and mulberries. We would take a white sheet to the patch and shake the mulberries off. Mother used them in jams or in desserts for something sweet after supper.

Potatoes served warm in their jackets with sour cream were a favorite when I was growing up, and later in my own household with our children. When I was a child, Mother would take the cream off the top of the milk that had gone sour and make a sour cream from it. She added a little salt also. We children never questioned how something tasted, that was just the way we had to eat it.

Sometimes Mother would fix pancakes or a simple chili soup for supper. At other times we had mashed potatoes, potato soup, or beef and noodles. We lived cheaply, but Mother always fixed good meals. I still remember when I first had Jell-O. I was a teenager and we had it at my aunt and uncle's one Sunday. We just didn't have the money to buy that kind of food back then. I also remember staying with our neighbors while Mother and Dad were out of town visiting relatives and they served store-bought salad dressing. They were better off than we were, because we never ate stuff like that. Those store-bought items were such a treat when I was growing up.

Meals were also simple at my grandma's. While she didn't have lots of different foods, she always had plenty of what she did have. Grandma would turn over a cardboard box on the floor with pretzels and candy on top for us to eat. All the grandchildren would sit around the box and eat the snacks—we thought that was great because we didn't get that much at home.

Sometimes we had goat meat, which was cheaper than hog meat. People don't raise goats for meat as much today, but there were a lot of people who butchered goats instead of hogs or beef back then. We'd fry the goat meat down in an iron kettle, then put it in a crock and pour lard on top to cover it. Then we'd heat it up for serving.

Later on, when Ben and I were first married, we didn't live high on the hog. When it was just Ben and I, we'd buy milk and it would sour on us because we didn't use it. I just fixed us potatoes and meat for supper, but we wouldn't even buy ham—we thought it was too expensive. We didn't butcher our own meat right from the start. We bought two cows from my dad in 1959 and then we had cows to milk. Then we had a couple of hogs. The first hog had fourteen pigs, which we butchered to have better meat. We made pork chops, hams, and bacon out of the hog, and steak out of the steer. What beef was left over we canned as chunks.

When Ben and I were raising our children we ate barbecued chicken, beef stew, ham, casseroles, plenty of vegetables from the garden, potatoes, and lots of other goodies. Eating

supper together is something Ben and I made sure we did with our children, and now that our children have families of their own, they also have supper together.

Our children enjoyed the meals that I fixed when they were still living at home. Our evening meals were filled with lots of singing and yodeling, and sometimes after supper, the children would go for a walk outside if it was nice. Other times the after-supper hours were spent writing letters and cards to faraway friends. During the summers, when it was lighter longer, sometimes we'd go out to the garden and hoe. There is always a lot of activity around here.

Since the Amish don't have phones, they'll often write letters to not-so-faraway people. I was amazed once when Elizabeth received a long letter in the mail from her daughter Emma, who lives just two miles away. Emma can put the letter in her mailbox in the morning and it will be delivered to Elizabeth several hours later. She still has to use a stamp, but that's pretty neat!

The Amish Cook

by Elizabeth Coblentz

June 1995

Those five birds in my Mother's Day flowerpot have hatched. It is interesting to see them taking advances from day to day. It looks like a little well-filled nest. One of these days they'll probably fly away. Sounds like there is a fuss out there at times. Such a perfect small nest in the middle of the hanging flowerpot.

Summer has arrived! We are having plenty of rain now; it has been stormy lately. Had hail last night. Garden goodies are doing great. We have radishes, lettuce, and onions galore. It is good to make all kinds of salads from the garden.

Friday, after the wedding of daughter Emma and Jacob, was a hectic day to get everything in place again. Furniture was put back in place and lots of dishes were put back in the cupboards and dishes that had to be washed yet, taking care of leftover food, benches put back in bench wagons and hauled away to where they belong. Then that Friday evening 633 bales of hay were brought in to be unloaded in the barn. There were some tired bodies going to bed. A long, hard day, but what a relief to see everything clean again.

Well I had best hurry as we are going to daughter Liz and husband Levi's to assist with her work, as church services were announced to be there Sunday. So there's lots to be done at such a time with two little ones to care for. A year ago she couldn't have church there as her baby was just born. Levi Jr. is a year old now. Daughter Lovina and Joe's daughter Elizabeth is a year old now, too. We gave little Elizabeth a couple of pieces of cake in the high chair for her birthday, but her little fingers didn't do the trick. It was all over her face; I guess she wanted to keep her fingers clean. Ha!

Some recipe totals from our wedding: We had fourteen plates of Amish Wedding Nothings (see page 148), thirty-eight bowls of Perfection Salad, and two gallons of Twenty-Four-Hour Cabbage Slaw. We also had lettuce with sliced radishes, shredded cheese, and bacon bits to top it with dressing. Had plenty of lettuce from the garden.

Here's a couple of recipes that we had at our wedding. Women folks done a good job with our food; the dishes were looking just like I like to see them. Pies looked so nice too.

Perfection Salad

Serves 4 to 6

1 (3-ounce) box orange Jell-O
1 teaspoon sugar
1 cup boiling water
1 cup cold water
1/2 cup peeled and shredded carrots
1/2 cup canned crushed pineapple, drained

Mix together the Jell-O and sugar in a 9-inch glass pie plate. Add the boiling water and stir for at least 2 minutes, until fully dissolved. Stir in the cold water and refrigerate for 35 to 40 minutes, uncovered, until the Jell-O has set to a point between liquid and solid but is not fully firm. Add the carrots and pineapple. (Adding the carrots and pineapple at this stage will cause the heavier pineapple to sink to the bottom and the lighter carrots to stay on top. The salad will have a colorful orange kaleidoscope look.) Do not stir. Refrigerate until firm.

Twenty-Four-Hour Cabbage Slaw

Serves 6

1/2 head cabbage, coarsely chopped
2 onions, coarsely chopped
1 green bell pepper, seeded and coarsely chopped
2 red bell peppers, seeded and coarsely chopped
1 cup apple cider vinegar
11/4 cups sugar
1/2 teaspoon salt
1/8 teaspoon turmeric
3/4 teaspoon mustard seed
1/2 teaspoon celery seed

Grind the cabbage, onions, and peppers in a hand-grinder (or pulse in an electric food processor) until medium ground. In a saucepan, bring the vinegar, sugar, salt, and spices to a boil. Mix everything together in a serving bowl, cover, and let stand in a cold cellar or refrigerator for 24 hours before serving.

While often sliced and served for supper, fresh bread can be found on the table at any meal of the day. I used to make a lot more bread when all of our children were still living at home—usually about nine loaves a week. It was so handy to have fresh bread when the children got home from school. I would bake the bread before they came so when they got in the door it was good and warm. They spread butter on it for a nice after-school snack. I've always just made white bread, but my sister Lovina and her daughter sometimes make brown bread using whole-wheat flour.

Home-baked bread spoils quicker than boughten bread, but it tastes better. I store home-baked bread in plastic bags. If the bread is sealed while still warm, it will stay fresh longer. It takes awhile to get the feel for making bread. My mother taught me how to bake bread and I taught my daughters. The instructions get passed down from generation to generation, so each family's recipe may be slightly different.

Homemade Bread

Makes 2 loaves

1 (^{1}/4-ounce) package active dry yeast

^{1}/2 cup plus 2 cups warm water or milk

1 heaping tablespoon lard or shortening

2 tablespoons sugar

1 tablespoon salt

7 to 8 cups all-purpose flour

In a small bowl, dissolve the yeast in the ^{1}/2 cup warm water. In a large mixing bowl, combine the lard, sugar, salt, and the remaining 2 cups water. Into the mixing bowl, stir the yeast and enough of the flour to make a soft, elastic dough that doesn't stick to the sides of the bowl. Cover the dough with a loose piece of cheesecloth or plastic wrap and let rise till double (about 1^1/4 hours) in a warm, draft-free place, such as a table close to the stove or a sunny windowsill. Punch the dough down, and divide it into 2 balls. Form 2 loaves with your hands. Put the loaves in greased loaf pans. Cover with a damp cloth and let rise again until double (45 to 60 minutes). Bake in a 325° oven for about 45 minutes. The bread will sound hollow when it's done. After removing the bread from the oven, brush the top with butter or margarine. This will make for a softer crust.

Sometimes people confuse this with the frozen, store-bought pot pies, but this is a very different, much older recipe. Pennsylvania Pot Pie Soup is another one of the simpler soups that tastes good and is hearty, but was available to make during harder times. This pot pie soup is a lot like a One-Kettle Soup (see page 60). We usually had our pot pie soup on Saturday.

Sometimes Mother would take pieces of cooked ham off the bone and add them to the soup. We use a pressure cooker to cook the ham bone. The length of cooking time depends on the age of the bone. A younger bone will cook in 30 to 35 minutes under 15 pounds of pressure. An older bone will take longer, about 45 minutes. Because we butcher our own hogs we always know the age of the bone. If you don't know the age, just cook it for 35 minutes.

My mother was taught by the older folks of her time to eat these soups. Unless I fix them, a lot of the younger children today will never taste these soups. Times are just better now.

Pennsylvania Pot Pie Soup

Serves 4 to 6

1 ham bone

12 cups plus 1 1/2 cups water

1 egg

2 cups all-purpose flour

3 potatoes, peeled and diced

Salt

Pepper

Cook the ham bone in a 6-quart pressure cooker half-filled with water (about 12 cups) under 15 pounds of pressure until soft, about 35 minutes. While cooking the ham bone, crack the egg into a bowl and stir in the remaining 1 1/2 cups water. Add the flour and mix until you have a smooth, elastic dough. Roll thin and cut into squares.

When the ham is done, scrape the meat from the bone and remove the bone from the pressure cooker. Add the potatoes and boil (without pressure) for 10 to 12 minutes over medium heat until fork tender. With the water still boiling, drop the dough squares into the pot and cook for 5 minutes after the last square is added. Season with salt and pepper to your taste.

Hint: The ham bone may also be cooked in an open kettle (without pressure) over low heat until soft, about 3 hours. Diced carrots can also be added.

Amish lore says that on an Amish woman's wedding day, the mother of the bride gives some sourdough starter to her daughter. The young bride then uses the starter to make bread for her new husband and eventually, her own family, later passing some of the same starter on to her daughters on their wedding day. In this way the bread gets passed from generation to generation. Although this practice still exists in some remote Amish communities, it seems to have died out in most.

This recipe for Friendship Bread is based on a sourdough starter made over a ten-day period. The starter is then given to three friends, along with the Friendship Bread recipe that follows the daily steps for making the starter.

Amish Friendship Bread

Makes 2 loaves

SOURDOUGH STARTER

5 1/2 cups all-purpose flour

2 cups plus 1 tablespoon sugar

1 (1/4-ounce) package active dry yeast

2 cups warm water

2 cups milk

Combine 3 1/2 cups of the flour, 1 tablespoon of the sugar, and the yeast in a large bowl. Gradually add the warm water and beat with a wooden spoon until smooth. Cover with a loose piece of cheesecloth or plastic wrap and let stand in a warm, draft-free place for 1 day. Follow these steps to finish the starter:

Day 1: Do nothing to the starter.

Days 2, 3, and 4: Stir the starter gently with a wooden spoon once a day (10 strokes).

Day 5: Add 1 cup of the flour, 1 cup of the sugar, and 1 cup of the milk to the starter. Stir with a wooden spoon. Re-cover the mixture and set in a warm place.

Days 6, 7, 8, and 9: Stir the starter gently with a wooden spoon once a day (10 strokes).

Day 10: Add the remaining 1 cup flour, 1 cup sugar, and 1 cup milk to the starter. Stir with a wooden spoon.

You'll know the starter (some call the completed form a "sponge") is done when it has a pleasant, sweet taste; the texture is creamy (not gritty); there is no flour taste; and the sponge is pourable and flows back together slowly on the back of a spoon.

Divide the starter into three 1-cup containers and give to three friends with these instructions:

FRIENDSHIP BREAD

1 cup sourdough starter

2/3 cup vegetable oil

2 cups all-purpose flour

3 eggs

2 teaspoons ground cinnamon

1 teaspoon vanilla extract

1/2 teaspoon salt

1/2 teaspoon baking soda

1 (5-ounce) box instant vanilla pudding mix

1 cup chopped nuts

Preheat the oven to 350°. Combine all of the ingredients in a large bowl and mix well with a wooden spoon (do not use metal). Pour the dough into 2 well-greased and floured loaf pans and bake for 40 to 50 minutes. Cover with foil toward the end of the baking time to prevent burning. Bread is done when a toothpick inserted into the center comes out clean. Cool in pans for 10 minutes and then remove from the pans and cover loosely to cool completely.

Hint: You can also bake this bread in a bundt pan; the cooking time remains the same.

When Mother did have meat in the house, like right after butchering day, she would make a good beef stew. Other times we'd have vegetable or chili soup made with fresh garden vegetables, or soup with beef or chicken noodles. During the hot summers, Mother poured cold milk over strawberries, raspberries, sugar, and cubed bread. If we didn't have meat around the house, Mother made Knepfle. I like to serve this with crackers or bread.

Knepfle

Serves 4 to 6

2 cups all-purpose flour

1/2 teaspoon salt

1/2 teaspoon baking powder

1 egg

1 1/2 cups water

4 cups chicken or beef broth or water

Combine the flour, salt, and baking powder in a bowl. In a separate bowl, beat the egg with the water. Add to the dry ingredients and mix into a crumbly dough. Pour the broth into a 3-quart saucepan and bring to a boil over medium-high heat. Hold the bowl with the dough over the boiling broth and drop the dough into the broth in small pieces from your spoon. Dip the spoon in the broth often to prevent the dough from sticking. Let the dough cook for 5 minutes, until the soup is thick and white in color. Serve hot.

When I was a girl, many times we didn't have enough meat for the evening supper. Mother would save what little meat we had for Dad, since he was working, and prepare other foods that were hearty for us. Mother taught us so many different ways to save, and I think that helped all of her children in later years. She always said, "It's not what you earn, it's what you save." We were brought up on these simple soups, but children today might not like them as much. We just ate whatever Mother fixed.

When times were especially tough, Mother would make rivvels. Rivvels are rice-sized pieces of dough served in soup that resembles gravy. Mother took the dough and rubbed it through her hands to drop it into a boiling broth. When we didn't have noodles, Mother would fix a warm, slightly spiced broth. We had rivvels a lot on Saturday because it was a good, inexpensive meal to eat before the larger, better meal on Sunday.

German Rivvel Soup

Serves 4 to 6

4 cups beef broth

1 cup all-purpose flour

1/4 teaspoon salt

1 egg, well beaten

Heat the broth in a pot until boiling. In a bowl, combine the flour, salt, and egg until the mixture is crumbly. Rub the dough through your hands into the boiling broth. Cook for about 10 minutes over medium heat. The rivvels will look like boiled rice when cooked.

Hint: You may also use milk instead of broth if you wish.

Even when times were tight, we always had potatoes on the table. When I was still living at home, our main potato meal was lightly salted potatoes served warm in their jackets. Nowadays, mashed potatoes are the favorite potato meal. We like to dip them onto a plate and eat them with gravy and noodles. Mother used to make a brown flour gravy by browning flour and lard and then adding cold water and some of the potato water. The flour made a thick gravy, and she liked it thick. I prefer gravy on the thin side, so instead of using flour, I make gravy with cornstarch, potato water, and a chicken soup base.

If stored on ice or in a refrigerator, mashed potatoes will last a couple of days. We add cream cheese to the potatoes to help keep them firm and fresh when being served to lots of people.

Delicious Mashed Potatoes

Serves 6

5 pounds potatoes, peeled and cut into quarters

4 ounces cream cheese

1/4 cup margarine or butter

3 cups milk

Salt

In a large kettle, boil the potatoes in water to cover. When the potatoes are soft, drain the water and place the potatoes in a large bowl. Mash them well. Add the cream cheese and margarine and mix well. Heat the milk until it is good and warm, but not boiling. Stir the milk into the potatoes. Add salt to your taste and serve hot.

Holy Communion services are held twice a year. The Communion service is slightly longer than a normal church service. Church members divide into groups of men and women and participate in a foot-washing ritual. Towels are set out for people to dry themselves off. The Communion wafer is a tiny piece of home-baked bread. A sip of wine from a dark brown, unlabeled bottle is offered to each member, symbolizing the blood of Christ.

Homemade catsup from the garden is so full of flavor. Although a lot of the younger people now prefer boughten catsup, I prefer homemade because you know for certain what's in it. You can never be sure what's in something you buy in a store.

Tomatoes are plentiful in our garden during the summer, so making homemade catsup is always easy. Most years we put out over ninety tomato plants, and I like a good variety of tomatoes. My favorites are Beefsteak, Big Boy, and Big Girl tomatoes. Beefsteak tomatoes are thick, hearty, and non-acidic, and do very well under the warm Indiana sun. Beefsteaks are big tomatoes—they can be eight inches across. The Big Boy and Big Girl tomatoes, which work well in this catsup recipe, also make good tomato chunks, which you can serve in tacos and in casseroles. Ben always liked orange tomatoes, which are called Jubilees. We use Jubilees for slicing, and they taste good on sandwiches. We also grow Rutgers tomatoes, a juicier variety that is good in homemade tomato and V-8–style juices, and in catsup.

You can drain off the juice that is created while making catsup and use it in from-scratch chicken or vegetable soup. I have plenty of homemade catsup canned in glass pint jars in my basement. I like my tomatoes good and ripe, on the soft side.

Tomato Catsup

Makes 7 to 9 cups

1 gallon chopped tomatoes

1 large onion, chopped

1 tablespoon pickling spice

2 teaspoons salt

1 cup sugar

1 cup apple cider vinegar

Cook the tomatoes with the onion and pickling spice in a large kettle over high heat for 20 to 30 minutes, until tomatoes are soft. Drain off the juice. Put the tomatoes and onions through a sieve and add the salt, sugar, and vinegar. Cook over high heat until the mixture is nice and thick, about 30 minutes. Pour into glass pint jars and seal.

Hint: This catsup will be thinner and more runny than store-bought.

We always made our own noodles when I was still living at home. Mother and us girls rolled the dough out into big circles and sliced the noodles by hand with a sharp butcher knife. We tried to keep them evenly cut, so we didn't have one big noodle and one small noodle. Now we have a hand-cranked noodle maker that rolls out and cuts the dough for us. What used to take all day now just takes a couple of hours. We can put 30 eggs, 30 tablespoons of water, and 30 cups of flour through the noodle maker in an hour, which cuts the whole process by more than half.

We put the noodles on a table or clothes rack to dry. The noodles take about a week to dry, but they need to be stirred up every day so they don't get sticky. I like to put yellow cake coloring in the dough because it makes a nice yellow noodle. We usually make noodles in the late fall or early spring when the weather is pleasant and the flies aren't around. We store our noodles in tightly sealed six-gallon cans. When you put them in sealed containers they will last for at least half a year, but the noodles have to be good and dry when you put them into the containers. We use noodles in lots of soups and casseroles. They taste even better when reheated.

Amish Noodles

Makes 1 pound

3 cups all-purpose flour

3 eggs

3 tablespoons water

$1/8$ teaspoon salt

Put the flour into a small bowl and make a well in the center. Drop the eggs, water, and salt into the well. Using your hands, mix the liquid with the flour, starting from the center and moving to the outside of the well, until a stiff dough is formed. Divide the dough in half and set one half aside. Roll the dough as thin as possible, about $1/16$ inch thick.

Lightly dust the top of the dough with flour. Roll the dough up into a log. Cut the log into $1/2$-inch-wide strips. Unroll the strips and lay them on a drying rack or cookie sheet. Follow the same steps for the remaining dough. Let the noodles air dry for 1 hour, turn them over, and let them dry for 1 additional hour. Keep the noodles on the drying rack and let them dry for 1 week. Rearrange the noodles on the drying rack every day to ensure they dry out evenly.

Summer is a time of slow solitude on the Coblentz farm. The season contrasts greatly with spring, a high-energy time of preparing the garden for planting, sowing seeds, gathering dandelion greens, anticipating June weddings, cleaning the house, and reawakening after winter. Fall is an equally busy time of canning, harvesting, collecting firewood, and stocking up for the long winter. Summer is a time to relax while waiting for the fruits of the spring's labor to blossom into a bountiful garden. When evening arrives and lightning flashes on the distant horizon, the stillness of the day succumbs to a chorus of cicadas. Sometimes I just want to pitch a tent on Elizabeth's lawn and never leave.

The Amish Cook

by Elizabeth Coblentz

September 1995

It is a breezy morning as I start writing this. After the 90 degrees we experienced yesterday, this weather feels refreshing. We could use a good shower again as this sure is hay fever season. Whoever suffers from it knows what I mean. My husband is bothered with it every year.

Saturday my husband and I attended the big event, which was *The Budget* gathering. *The Budget* (a weekly newspaper) in Sugarcreek, Ohio, is now 105 years old. It carries letters from Amish people all over; without telephones it is often the sole source of long-distance communication for us. Forty-three years ago, I took up the task of writing for *The Budget,* describing our area news. With Amish people moving to new areas all the time, it has become a big weekly paper.

A good dinner was served to all the scribes (scribes are people who write for the weekly paper). The food and fellowship were great. The meal consisted of mashed potatoes, gravy, fried chicken, roast beef, dressing, corn, salad, pie, Pepsi, coffee, tea, bread, and butter.

The person writing for *The Budget* the longest was an Amish woman who has been writing for seventy-one years. She is from the state of Delaware and was not able to attend the reunion in Sugarcreek. Around three hundred people attended. The last gathering was five years ago, when the newspaper celebrated its centennial.

We left at 3:00 A.M. on Saturday morning and were back home by 10:15 P.M. Saturday night. Had an enjoyable day!

You may wonder whether we traveled to Sugarcreek by horse and buggy. No, it would've been too hard on the horse for a whole day. But our brother-in-law once made the three hundred–mile trip from our place to Sugarcreek with horses and a buggy. They were surprised how many friendly people they met along the way, offering them food and water and feed for their horses. A friend of ours took us in their van to Ohio. Joe and Lovina and their baby went with us and visited their relatives out there in those hills of Holmes County, Ohio, while we attended the gathering.

Will share some recipes. Some might be in their canning season and harvesting their fresh peaches.

Fresh Peach Custard Pie

Makes 1 (8-inch) pie

*1 (8-inch) unbaked Never-Fail Pie Crust
    (see page 127)*
*6 small fresh peeled peaches (about
    1 pound), pitted and halved*
1 cup sugar
2 tablespoons butter, melted
2 eggs, lightly beaten
1/2 teaspoon vanilla extract

Preheat the oven to 350°. Roll out the crust and line an 8-inch pie pan, as directed on page 127. Arrange the peaches in a single layer, pit-side down, in the unbaked pie shell. In a bowl, combine the sugar, butter, eggs, and vanilla. Pour over the peaches. Bake for 50 minutes, until the pie is brown and crusty on top. The center should be set and the peaches should be tender when pierced with a fork.

Hint: Cooking time may be longer if you are using larger peaches.

Garden Corn Relish

Makes about 5 cups

4 cups sweet corn
2 tablespoons diced green cabbage
1^1/2 teaspoons finely diced onion
1^1/2 teaspoons finely diced green
    bell pepper
1^1/2 teaspoons finely diced red
    bell pepper
1 heaping tablespoon all-purpose flour
^{1}/4 cup plus ^{1}/2 teaspoon apple cider
    vinegar
^{1}/8 teaspoon freshly ground turmeric
^{1}/4 teaspoon dry mustard
2^1/8 teaspoons celery seed
^{1}/8 teaspoon mustard seed
^{1}/8 teaspoon salt
1^1/2 teaspoons sugar
1^1/2 teaspoons water

In a saucepan, combine the corn, cabbage, onion, and peppers. In a separate bowl, combine the flour and ^{1}/2 teaspoon vinegar and mix until smooth. Add the turmeric, mustard, celery seed, mustard seed, salt, sugar, water, and the remaining ^{1}/4 cup vinegar and pour over the vegetables. Cook over low heat for 30 minutes. Put into sterilized glass jars and seal.

Leftovers

When you prepare too much food at a meal, the question of what to do with all the leftovers inevitably arises. Here are some helpful ways to make use of them.

* *Leftover noodles may be added to vegetable soup or leftover meat and vegetable dishes.*

* *Leftover meat, potatoes, gravy, and any kind of vegetable may be placed in layers in a pan or casserole dish. Add meat broth, tomato juice, or spices, and heat.*

* *Leftover chicken can be made into a macaroni casserole. Cook some macaroni until soft, then mix it with diced chicken and gravy. Put everything in a baking dish. Add milk to cover the macaroni, and season with salt and pepper. Top the dish with breadcrumbs or crushed saltine crackers, and bake for 20 to 30 minutes at 350°.*

* *Leftover potatoes can be made into delicious patties. Add 2 eggs to a cup of mashed potatoes and mix. Drop the mixture by tablespoonfuls onto a greased skillet. When brown on one side, turn over and let brown on the other side.*

We have several apple trees growing in our yard. They supply us with enough apples for applesauce, baked apples, apple dumplings, apple crisps, and sliced apples, which are all enjoyable snacks around here. Each type of apple has its best use. MacIntosh apples are good cooking apples served warm at dinner or in a pie. Jonathan apples are tart and taste best around Christmastime when they've gotten soft. Jonathan and MacIntosh apples will keep through the winter if stored in a cool cellar.

A yellow apple works best for applesauce. We pick these in the fall and store them in the cellar so they are ripe and ready for applesauce by the early spring. I don't like to can too many apples at one time because I want to have fresh applesauce from year to year. New strainers have made the job of making homemade applesauce easier. Some years, when there is a late spring frost, the trees just don't give as many apples and we miss them.

Applesauce

9 yellow apples

$^1/3$ cup sugar

Peel, core, and roughly chop the apples, then place them in a 2-quart saucepan. Cover and cook over medium heat until the apples are mushy, about 5 minutes. Mash the apples with a potato masher, then add the sugar. Let set for 3 minutes. Serve the applesauce warm.

Hint: Leftover applesauce can be chilled and served with other meals.

Our apple trees were planted in 1971 and they are still going strong. We fertilize them with equal parts Epsom salts, wood ashes, and lime, which we put around the roots of the trees in the spring.

Barn Raisings

When the day of a barn raising is upon us, we wonder how many people will come. The count could be several hundred, with at least 75 or more menfolk and boys to assist. In large Amish communities there could be 100 to 140 or more menfolk to put up the framework of the barn in one day.

On the day of the barn raising, the men arrive at dawn with their nail aprons, hammers, tape measures, saws, and squares. A lot of the men take their toolboxes along so that they have a variety of tools on hand—whatever they need. These tools will be used throughout the day. The men are divided into groups with a leader who will show his crew what has to be done. I think it's a dangerous job if one's not careful enough.

The barn-raising crews usually have the barn under roof by evening. Some barn raisings can be finished in one day's time, but some of the larger barns can't be finished in one day. Enough can be put up so that a smaller group of family and friends can finish the rest on another day. The size of the barn depends on what the family wants. Some people have more cattle, so they need more barn space.

It's remarkable to watch a barn raising, to see how the

barn takes shape. I've been to several in my lifetime, including our own barn raising when I was still young. I must have been about ten years old. To see the menfolk put the frame together and the siding and roof on is quite a memory. It was completed in a day, but it began raining in the evening. I still remember that there were 126 people—women and children included—who came to help that day. We thought at the time that 126 was a lot, but compared to nowadays it is not. There are more people around today, so we might have as many as 250 show up.

A snack of coffee, cookies, and cold drinks is served to all the men, women, and children in the forenoon. At noon, we serve a good dinner of desserts, casseroles, baked goods, and you name it. Long tables are set up in the yard where shade is available, and the food is set on the tables. The tables give the women a place to set the food and provide a makeshift place to eat the meal. The food is served cafeteria-style.

In the afternoon, another snack, like cold lemonade and cookies, is passed to all present. The boys especially enjoy the break. The snack is taken to them after the dishes have been cleared at noon. In the late afternoon, the workers are served a cold drink to quench their thirst on a hot day. Women are usually kept busy caring for the small children.

We grow a lot of cucumbers in our garden, and Mother also grew a lot in hers. I think pickles taste better if you wait until you have a big, full-grown cucumber. Like with my tomatoes, I like to grow a variety of cucumbers. The Burpee variety is long and thin with fewer seeds, so these are my favorite.

There are so many ways to fix cucumbers. I like a salad with cucumbers from the garden, as well as sweet pickles, refrigerator pickles, and homemade pickles made with vinegar, sugar, salt, and pickling spice. We can cucumbers and eat them fresh with salad dressing and a variety of snacks. Jacob likes to eat them with onions and vinegar, just sliced with salt, and even over baked potatoes. For a quick cucumber snack like the kind Jacob enjoys, just slice the cucumbers and coat each side lightly with vinegar. Serve cold in a bowl with diced onions and diced tomatoes.

No summertime supper table would be complete without fried cucumbers.

Rachel's Fried Cucumbers

Serves 4 to 6

4 large cucumbers, peeled and sliced lengthwise 3/4-inch thick

2 cups all-purpose flour

1/2 cup lard or shortening for frying

Salt

Pepper

Roll the cucumbers in the flour until they are lightly covered on all sides. Melt the lard in a large frying pan over high heat then fry the cucumbers until golden on all sides. Salt and pepper to your taste.

Elizabeth's garden, situated in the sometimes shadow of a creaking old windmill, is the same one she's tilled for almost fifty years.

When someone needs a new barn in our area, we have a barn raising. The men are divided into teams by a head man, who is an experienced carpenter. Some of the teams put the rafters up and others hold the ropes. Each team has their certain job. Barn raisings in small communities have fewer people participating than in large communities. There were about fifty men and boys helping to put up the barn at the last one I attended.

A light salad that you can prepare the night before is a good thing to serve during the dinner break at a barn raising. Make this good bean salad twenty-four hours before serving.

Three-Bean Salad

Serves 4 to 6

SALAD

2 cups fresh or 1 (16-ounce) can green beans, cut into 1-inch pieces

2 cups fresh or 1 (16-ounce) can yellow waxed beans, cut into 1-inch pieces

1 (16-ounce) can kidney beans, washed and drained

1 cup chopped and seeded green bell pepper

1 1/2 cups chopped celery

1 cup chopped onion

DRESSING

2/3 cup honey

1/2 cup vegetable oil

3/4 cup apple cider vinegar

1/2 teaspoon salt

Place the fresh green and yellow waxed beans in a medium saucepan and cover with 1 quart of water (it's not necessary to cook the beans if using canned). Cook over medium heat for 20 minutes, until the beans are tender but firm. Drain and cool. Combine the cooked beans and the kidney beans with the green pepper, celery, and onion in a large bowl. Put the honey, oil, vinegar, and salt in a covered jar and shake well. Pour the dressing over the salad and stir gently. Refrigerate overnight. Stir the salad several times before serving.

The Amish Cook

by Elizabeth Coblentz

September 1995

The first frost brushed the tops of late summer melons with ice. Amazing to have a first frost this early. This week has been full of little problems, but I guess I should not complain. Our health has been good and there is plenty of food for the table. Guess we should thank our Creator for such blessings.

We spent last evening tending to Mae. Mae has been my horse for twenty years. Yesterday she injured her leg while pulling my buggy into town; she twisted her ankle in a rut in the road. She went down fast; luckily it happened close to home and she was able to limp back. The Amish herb doctor prescribed a mixture of liquid vitamins, hoping that would make her snap out of it. Ben says she'll probably have to be shot. She is suffering, but I hate to see her go, she was such a dependable horse for all these years. I guess life has its share of upsets. So that is taking all the attention around here.

Today, Susan and I were going to put a quilt in frame. Just as we prepared the frame and were going to quilt a peach-colored quilt, we realized that we were out of peach-colored thread. We want to finish a quilt sometime this month; they are so nice and warm for the long winter months ahead.

My aged mother is staying with us this week. She gets very good care when she stays with us. Daughter Emma sewed her a brand new dress last night, and daughter Lovina is preparing her favorite meals. Mother doesn't eat as much as she used to. Her favorite meals are simple ones: coffee soup and bread soups. She likes to break up bread in a cup and pour coffee over it and eat it.

We get our water from a pump inside a water closet in our kitchen. The water comes from a ground well. The handle on the pump broke yesterday morning. So all the girls had to go outside and wash their hair, it was a little too chilly for that! Ben says it should be fixed by tomorrow morning. We have a water pump outside that is powered by our windmill; that water also comes from a ground well.

Susan and I made some Elephant Ears for the grandchildren. They love them; a little bit messy, but delicious!

Elephant Ears

Makes 24 elephant ears

Dough

1 (1/4-ounce) package active dry yeast
1/4 cup warm water
2 cups all-purpose flour
1 cup plus 2 tablespoons sugar
1/2 teaspoon salt
1/3 cup margarine or butter
1/3 cup milk
1 egg, beaten
1/4 teaspoon ground cinnamon for coating

Topping

3/4 cup firmly packed brown sugar
1/4 cup margarine or butter, softened
1/4 cup finely chopped pecans

To make the dough, dissolve the yeast in the warm water. Combine the flour, 2 tablespoons of the sugar, and salt in a large bowl. Cut in the margarine until the mixture resembles coarse meal. Add the dissolved yeast, milk, and egg. Set aside, uncovered, to rise till puffy, about 30 minutes.

Preheat the oven to 400°. Separate the dough into 24 equal pieces shaped roughly like the palm of your hand. In a small bowl, combine the remaining sugar and the cinnamon and sprinkle evenly over a cutting board. Roll each piece of dough in the sugar mixture (both sides) until very thin and 3 to 5 inches in diameter. Place on a well-greased baking sheet about 1/2 inch apart.

To make the topping, mix together the brown sugar, margarine, and pecans in a bowl. The mixture will be crumbly. Sprinkle the topping over the elephant ears. This spreads fast once baking begins so don't put too much on. Bake until light brown and topping has spread, about 8 to 10 minutes. Remove immediately and serve warm.

When a barn raising is held, sometimes the woman of the house will have a quilt in frame so the women can quilt while the men work. Each woman brings her own thimbles and scissors along. Barn raisings begin at daybreak and last until almost dark, so there's plenty of time for quilting. Sixteen to twenty women can be seated around a quilt frame at once. Lots of stitches go on a quilt on such a day.

While some women are quilting, others are watching the children, and still others are preparing the noon meal. The meal is prepared in the kitchen of the house where the barn is being raised. Usually we bring the meal outside, but if the weather is bad, we all eat indoors. Serving a hearty casserole like this is a perfect way to get the menfolk through the hard work ahead.

Hamburger Casserole

2 pounds freshly ground beef

1 (16-ounce) can tomato sauce

1 cup cooked white rice

1/4 cup chopped onion

3/4 cup chopped and seeded green bell pepper

1 tablespoon chili powder

1/2 teaspoon salt

1/2 teaspoon pepper

2 cups shredded Cheddar or Colby cheese

Preheat the oven to 350°. Brown the ground beef in a skillet. Drain the excess grease and remove from the heat. In a 3-quart casserole dish, mix together the beef, tomato sauce, rice, onion, green pepper, chili powder, salt, pepper, and 1 cup of the cheese. Spread the remaining 1 cup cheese over the top and bake for 20 minutes, until the cheese melts and the casserole is hot throughout.

Summer Evenings

Summer is a generous time with limpid nights, the sound of crickets, and fireflies with their miniature lights darting above us in the dusk. There are so many tasks to be done in the summer, and as long there's daylight, we find plenty of work to do. During the hottest days of summer, we often do our hoeing and weeding after the sun goes down. It is easier to work in the garden when it is cooler, and the cry of the bobwhite can be heard as we work.

While working outside in the warmth, we naturally encounter bugs. We hate to use chemicals in our yard, so we use a homemade remedy to get rid of the bugs: Take an empty plastic soda bottle, add 1 cup of sugar, 1 cup of vinegar, and a banana peel. Fill the bottle three-fourths full of water and hang it uncovered in a tree. It may take a week for the trap to start attracting bugs, but once it does, you'll find this to be a very effective way to take care of the problem. It collects all kinds of insects.

Sometimes we are invited to someone's house to enjoy an evening meal, so that gives us a rest. Other times we have company come over, which ends our workday early. Croquet, kickball, and straight-base—a simpler, homemade version of baseball—are popular outdoor games among the Amish in our community. When the girls were all

still living at home, they would go horseback (bareback) riding in the fields. We had a pony named Ginger that we bought for ten cents from a neighbor. She lived for over twenty years and was great with the children. The girls would hook Ginger up to a homemade pony-cart and take rides down the road.

There wasn't nearly as much automobile traffic on the roads back then. When Amos and Albert were in the fields making hay, the girls would take them water or a snack with Ginger and the cart. And Albert once made an outside playhouse for the girls that had a tea set, dishes, and some tea spices from the garden.

Riding home from errands in town on our horse-drawn buggy is pleasant when the first cool breezes of evening bring in the night. The countryside gently passes to the slow rhythm of the horse's hooves. We sing and yodel as we drive along on nice, clear evenings. On rainy evenings up go our umbrellas to protect us from getting wet. In this part of Indiana our buggies don't have roofs on them. The umbrellas really do their duty, as do waterproof blankets to cover us as we are seated in our buggy seat. Rainy evenings give us a chance to get caught up with letter writing, reading, or other indoor chores.

Barn raisings are held at all times of the year, whenever someone needs a barn. Sometimes a barn burns down, someone loses one to a storm, or newlyweds need one after moving into a new home. One day my uncle was making hay and saw a storm coming up. He quickly got the hay into the barn so it wouldn't get wet, but then lightning struck the barn with all that new, dry hay inside. The barn burnt to the ground. As soon as everything was cleaned up, a barn raising was held.

This casserole is another dish that will provide enough energy for the hard-working carpenter crews to make it through to the barn's completion. The noon meal gives everyone a chance to take a needed break and do some social-izing. Like the Hamburger Casserole (see page 99), this cheesy meal is excel-lent fuel for the rest of the day. For thick sauce, use more cheese. For thin sauce, use less cheese.

Cheesy Casserole

1 1/2 pounds freshly ground beef

1 large onion, chopped

4 cups milk

1/2 cup all-purpose flour

2 cups grated American cheese

6 cups cooked and drained Amish Noodles (see page 87), or 1 (12-ounce) package cooked and drained store-bought noodles

2 cups fresh or frozen peas

Pinch of salt

Pinch of pepper

Preheat the oven to 350°. Brown the beef and onion over medium-high heat. Drain and set aside. Combine the milk and flour in a saucepan until smooth. Add the cheese and cook over low heat until the cheese has melted and the sauce has thickened. Pour the cheese sauce into a casserole dish and mix in the beef and onion, noodles, peas, and salt and pepper to your taste. Bake for 1 hour, until bubbly.

Once, on our way to daughter Leah's with the horse and buggy, one of the horse's shoes came off its foot and rolled back to the hind buggy wheel. The wheel caused the horseshoe to flip in the air and it landed back in the buggy box. We had never seen such a happening. It's lucky the horseshoe didn't hit anyone in the head.

As cheap as potatoes are nowadays, it is sometimes easier to buy them than to grow them, but homegrown potatoes have a better taste. We grow our own potatoes during the spring and summer, but we buy our winter supply from friends who sand-grow potatoes in Ohio. I think potatoes grown in sandy soil taste better. I also really like red potatoes, which have a sweet taste. We usually buy about a thousand pounds of potatoes, which will last from the fall to the spring. We store our potatoes in the cellar in crates or gunnysacks, and by spring there are some leftover winter potatoes that, by then, are little and shriveled. We stick those potatoes in the ground and have our own supply by summer. Emma cuts the small, shrively ones in two before she plants them, so she gets even more out of them.

Potatoes were on the menu almost every night when I was growing up, and I served them most nights to my own children as well. If you are looking for a change of pace from mashed potatoes or potatoes in their jackets, this casserole is a good one. Fresh, homegrown potatoes taste best in this casserole.

Ben's Favorite Potato Casserole

Serves 4 to 6

2 pounds potatoes, peeled and thinly sliced

2 1/2 cups Cream of Chicken Soup (see page 168), or 1 (10 3/4-ounce) can condensed cream of chicken soup plus 1 can water

1/2 cup melted butter

2 cups grated cheese (any kind)

1 teaspoon salt

2 cups sour cream

1/2 cup chopped onion

1 (4-ounce) package crackers, crushed

Preheat the oven to 350°. Mix together the potatoes, chicken soup, butter, cheese, salt, sour cream, and onion in a big bowl. Spoon the mixture into a 2-quart casserole dish. Sprinkle the cracker crumbs over the top and bake for 45 minutes, until the top is golden brown.

Winter Evenings

There are no dull evenings when our family is together. We don't have television or radio, but we always enjoy our evenings just the same. Being brought up without them, you just don't think about it, I guess. When we have company in the evening, the hours really speed up. During the winter, the Caroom board is often in use, as are Chinese checkers and Aggravation. Aggravation is our main game, but the menfolk and boys enjoy Caroom.

When the children were younger, my evenings were spent in front of my Singer sewing machine. The sewing machine would be singing while everyone else was in their peaceful sleep. My mind was clear to think then. As years went on, I couldn't sew at nighttime anymore. I often think of those bygone years and how a lot of evenings were spent keeping the clothes sewn for the children. Now our children have homes and children of their own. I still have two daughters who live at home. What would I do without them, especially during those cold winter months? One winter, when all of our girls except Leah were unmarried and living at home, we quilted five quilts plus several bed comforters. In the evenings, the five daughters and I would quilt till late. We were glad when all was completed. That's a winter I'll never forget.

Ben mostly enjoyed reading on those cold winter evenings. My daughter Lovina is also an avid reader. Otherwise, we might spend an evening washing dishes, singing songs, or yodeling. Thinking back, it was nice to have our eight children at home and in our care. Today, our married children and their families

still come often for supper and to spend the evening. They know that there is always a welcome sign on our door. Life would seem dull without the children and their families.

The perfect meal on a summer evening is pork chops, chicken, or beef cooked outside on the grill. We like to coat the chicken with a juicy, tangy marinade as it grills. My daughter Verena fixes a delicious chicken marinade using a 1-quart dipper three-fourths full of apple cider vinegar, a stick of melted butter, and salt and pepper to taste. When it's brushed over the chicken it makes for a delicious dinner.

Another of our favorites for a summer supper is a hamburger patty sandwich. We add cracker crumbs, eggs, and onions to the fresh ground beef. We use ground beef from our home-butchered steer, but good store-bought beef can also be used.

Hamburger Sandwiches

Serves 4 to 6

1/2 cup cracker crumbs

2 eggs, beaten

1 pound freshly ground beef

1 onion, chopped

Pinch of salt

Pinch of pepper

6 hamburger buns

6 slices tomato

6 leaves lettuce

In a bowl, stir the cracker crumbs and eggs into the ground beef. Stir in the onion. Season with salt and pepper. Form the ground beef into 6 (4-inch-wide and 1/2-inch-thick) patties and grill or pan-fry over medium heat until the bottom side is firm and brown. Turn over and continue grilling. Make a small cut with a paring knife, and when the meat is no longer red, the hamburger is done. Toast the buns and top each hamburger with a slice of tomato and lettuce, or whatever else you prefer.

When winter arrives, everyone spends the evening together, inside and away from the elements. How enjoyable! The barn chores are completed in the early evening, and the supper dishes are washed and put back in their usual place. Winter suppers are hearty, balanced, late-day meals. Yummasetti is a traditional Pennsylvania German dish, most common in Pennsylvania and Ohio Amish communities, but a favorite everywhere. Using homemade noodles, a taste of sour cream, and lots of care, this is a perfect supper for a cold winter's night. We use homemade bread and from-scratch soups in this recipe, but it will turn out very good using boughten ingredients also.

Yummasetti

5 slices white bread

$1/4$ cup butter

$1^1/2$ pounds freshly ground beef

1 small onion, diced

6 cups cooked and drained Amish Noodles (see page 87), or 1 (12-ounce) package cooked and drained store-bought noodles

1 cup fresh or frozen peas

$2^1/2$ cups Cream of Mushroom Soup (see page 168), or 1 (10$^3/4$-ounce) can condensed cream of mushroom soup plus 1 can water

$1^1/2$ cups Cream of Chicken Soup (see page 168), or $1/2$ (10$^3/4$-ounce) can condensed cream of chicken soup plus $1/2$ can water

$1/2$ cup sour cream

1 cup shredded Cheddar cheese for topping

Toast the bread slices to golden brown and cut into small cubes. Melt the butter and toss with the bread cubes in a bowl. Set aside. Fry the ground beef and onion in a skillet over medium heat until browned, about 15 minutes. Preheat the oven to 350°. In a 2-quart casserole dish, layer the noodles, ground beef and onion, and peas. Pour the soups evenly over the layers. Drop the sour cream by teaspoonfuls evenly over the mixture. Sprinkle the bread cubes on top. Cover with foil and bake for 50 minutes. Remove the foil and sprinkle with the cheese. Return to the oven and bake for 10 minutes more. Serve hot.

Our winter evenings are spent in so many ways. If we have some of the family here for supper, afterwards we will sit around the stove and munch on freshly popped popcorn. We serve fresh apples and homemade apple cider, which are both a treat for us and for any family who is visiting. There are various kinds of games to play, along with singing, yodeling, and talking about the events of the day. Sometimes, on quieter winter evenings, I'll write "The Amish Cook" column for the newspapers while the girls catch up on letter writing. Our writing is done by the light of a well-lit lamp or lantern. This recipe for Wigglers, like the Yummasetti (see page 105), is a common Pennsylvania German dish. It's homemade and hearty.

Wigglers

3 slices bacon

1 pound freshly ground beef

1 large onion, diced

1/2 pound thin spaghetti

1 large potato

3/4 cup shaved carrot

3/4 cup finely diced celery

1 cup fresh or frozen peas

1 cup Cream of Mushroom Soup (see page 168), or 1/2 (10 3/4-ounce) can condensed cream of mushroom soup plus 1/2 can water

2 cups Fresh Tomato Soup (see page 169), or 1 (10 3/4-ounce) can condensed tomato soup plus 1 can water

Preheat the oven to 350°. Fry the bacon in a skillet over medium heat until crisp. Remove the bacon from the skillet and set aside to drain on a paper towel. Fry the ground beef and onion in the bacon grease until browned, about 15 minutes. While frying the ground beef, cook the spaghetti in a pot of boiling water until tender (about 6 minutes) and drain. In a separate pot, cover the potato with water and cook over medium heat for 10 minutes, until tender but firm. Peel and cube the potato. Put the ground beef and onion in the bottom of a 2-quart casserole dish and cover with the potatoes, carrot, celery, and peas. Pour the mushroom soup over the vegetables. Stir gently, mixing the mushroom soup throughout. Add the cooked spaghetti and crumble the bacon over the top. Add the tomato soup and stir. Bake, covered with foil, for 45 minutes. Remove the foil and bake for 15 minutes more, until the top is brown and crusty.

The Amish Cook

by Elizabeth Coblentz

February 1996

We had lots of snow this winter. Snowbound for awhile at some places. Some who left in the morning couldn't return back home in the evening. Such huge snowdrifts. Reminds me of back in the blizzard of '78—it was bad. That's when our children were still in our care. We could walk over fences and write our names on the shed roof. Drifts as high as ten feet. It was enjoyable back then, but now you think of the children at such a time. Just hoping no severe sickness or fire breaking out. So you see there's no end even if the children have their own household.

After our big snow last week the weather has turned warmer, melting the snow and exposing the ice underneath, making driving hard for the cars. The next experience was high water with more rain falling. Lots of roads unpassable around here. One little town in our area was enclosed with water. It got colder again and ice formed, so skating took place.

We helped son Albert butcher three hogs on Saturday. Always enjoyable to have the family work together. The fresh sausage is tasting yummy now on the table. They skinned the hogs after being shot. Some scald them in a butcher tank of hot water. Guess it's lots less work to carry water to the tank and keep fire underneath until hot, where the hogs are then shaven clean. They were hung on scaffolds and cut wide open and the stomach, etc., removed. The women then take care of the intestines, which are scraped clean. Scraping them twice will really make them clean. Sausage is ground through the meat grinder with various kinds of the meat. Then seasoned with salt and pepper. The women also cut up the fat in small pieces to be rendered into lard. Fresh lard has such a good smell when poured in cans for storage.

The women took care also to clean the stomach, tongue, brains, and intestines. The ribs were also cut up. Some like the brains of the hogs or cows, but this household isn't too fond of them. My parents used to buy brains at the store when we were in their care. Back then they tasted good. Probably there's lots better meat to prepare now than years ago. Guess we are all just living better than in our younger years. But those were the good old years. Lots of memories.

Will share a recipe sent to me by a reader:

Inexpensive Fruitcake

Makes 2 loaves

1 cup large, seedless raisins (cut in half)
1 cup dates, chopped
2 cups sugar
2 cups boiling water
5 tablespoons shortening
3 cups plus 1 teaspoon all-purpose flour
1 teaspoon baking soda
2 teaspoons ground cinnamon
1 teaspoon ground cloves
1 teaspoon salt
1 cup chopped nuts
1 cup mixed candied fruit

Preheat the oven to 325°. Place the raisins, dates, sugar, water, and shortening in a saucepan and simmer gently for 20 minutes. Remove from the heat and cool completely. Sift the 3 cups of flour and then sift again with the baking soda, cinnamon, cloves, and salt. Stir the flour mixture into the cooled raisin mixture until well blended. The batter will be thick.

In a separate bowl, toss the remaining 1 teaspoon flour with the nuts and candied fruit. Stir into the batter gently. Pour into 2 greased and floured loaf pans. Bake for 1 hour and 15 minutes, until a toothpick inserted into the center comes out clean.

CHAPTER 4

❋ ❋ ❋ ❋

Desserts

Mother taught me a lot about making desserts, and many of them my daughters and I still make to this day. Times were tight when I was growing up, so we didn't think about fixing desserts often, except for something simple like a fruit salad or prunes. Although cakes, pies, and cookies weren't common during tough times, Mother still taught us girls what desserts to fix. That's how recipes get passed down around here.

Some desserts, like Raisin Pie (see page 153), are saved for special occasions like weddings. Others, like homemade party mixes or popcorn, are simple and are enjoyed more often. We eat popcorn on cold winter evenings or on Sunday afternoons after church. We have an old three-quart popcorn popper that we use on top of the kerosene stove. The popper is filled with about an inch of melted lard left over from butchering our hogs. The popcorn kernels, which are stored in a sealed kitchen cookie jar, are scooped out and put into the popper. Once we have the fluffy white snack, we season it with popcorn salt or butter and cheese. It's delicious.

My oldest daughter, Leah, is the cookie baker in the family, although all my daughters know how to bake. Leah makes a lot of different cookies, from chocolate chip to snickerdoodles. My girls used to enjoy an icebox oatmeal cookie with their breakfast. Cookies get eaten quickly around here, especially with all of the grandchildren around.

From crunches and pies to cookies and spreads, there are many ways to have a sweet ending to a meal. This chapter has some of our family favorites.

The Amish Cook

by Elizabeth Coblentz

December 1996

Tuesday at 9:00 A.M. was the funeral of my aged, ninety-year-old mother. She peacefully fell asleep on Saturday, November 2, at 9:25 A.M. It's been a blessing that she could leave this wide, wicked world. She had longed to be in God's care since Dad's death, but there's a purpose for it all.

There were fifty-five or fifty-six horse and buggies and eight vans that went to the graveyard where dear mother was laid to rest. Dad was laid to rest seven years ago in the same graveyard. Dear parents are gone, but not forgotten. Mother left behind 7 living children, 80 grandchildren, and 302 great-grandchildren. She had her husband, a daughter, 5 grandchildren, and 7 great-grandchildren deceased. Mother came from a family of 15 and has 4 sisters living.

We were glad for the nice weather we had over the funeral. Meals were prepared in a shed and everyone ate out there. Everyone who attended the funeral was invited for dinner at noon, as that's the usual way. The funeral was largely attended. We'll miss her, but are glad she won't have to survive the cold winter ahead. Viewing was from Sunday evening until the time of services.

As if that wasn't all enough, my husband, Ben, has been under a doctor's care. Hasn't been well the last couple of weeks, but was glad he was able to go all those days before the funeral.

Otherwise, this is a nice autumn day. Looks like the trees in our nearby woods lost their colorful leaves. The trailer home across our driveway, that Joe and Lovina lived in for a couple of years, is now on wheels and one of these days it'll be moving out of our driveway. Lots of memories when Joe and Lovina and the two daughters lived in it.

I'll share something quick for this week's recipe.

Mother's Chicken Salad

Serves 4

4 cups diced cooked chicken
4 hard-boiled eggs, peeled and finely
chopped
2 cups diced celery
1/3 cup chopped pitted olives
1/2 teaspoon salt
1 cup Salad Dressing (see page 167) or
Miracle Whip
Lettuce leaves for serving

Toss the chicken, egg, celery, and olives together in a large bowl. Add the salt and stir. Add the salad dressing and mix well. Chill. Serve on lettuce leaves.

We usually make ice cream during the winter, when the water has frozen outside and ice is plentiful. It is so nice to eat ice cream on a cold winter night while sitting by the warm wood-burning stove. Most people in our community eat their home-made ice cream during the winter, but some also make it during the summer. I used to use the cream off the cans of milk when we were milking the cows—it made the best ice cream! We use a six-quart hand-cranked ice-cream freezer. I've never measured the ingredients, but I will make note of them for this recipe. It's sure to please everyone in the family, especially the grandchildren. We serve our ice cream in warm waffle cones or in bowls, sprinkled with fresh fruit.

Homemade Ice Cream

ICE CREAM

3 cups cream

9 cups milk

7 eggs

3 1/2 cups sugar

4 teaspoons vanilla extract

1 teaspoon salt

Ice

Rock salt

In the container of a hand-cranked or electric ice cream maker, combine the cream, milk, eggs, sugar, vanilla, and salt until smooth. Insert the container into the ice cream maker and fill the outside with 5 parts ice to 1 part rock salt. Crank (or turn on) the ice cream maker and process until the ice cream is thick.

Hint: Sometimes we pour a little hot water over the rock salt and ice; it freezes quicker that way.

I think rhubarb is easy to grow. Emma and Lovina put their rhubarb out when they moved into their own homes and got good results right away. Liz had a hard time growing hers when she first moved out on her own, but now hers grows fine. Ben didn't like rhubarb when we were first married. I made rhubarb jams and rhubarb shortcakes for him, but he would not eat it. One day the men he worked with brought him some rhubarb shortcake for dinner. He was afraid to refuse it for fear of being impolite, so he tried it. When I heard about it, I said, "Hey, if you can eat rhubarb someplace else then you can eat it here." So then Ben started eating and enjoying rhubarb. If someone in your family doesn't like the taste of rhubarb, try making a crunch like this one. It has a good, sweet cobbler flavor.

Rhubarb Crunch

Serves 4 to 6

1 cup granulated sugar

1 1/2 cups plus 3 tablespoons all-purpose flour

3 cups diced fresh rhubarb

1 cup firmly packed brown sugar

1 cup rolled oats

1/4 cup butter or shortening, softened

Warm milk or cream for serving

Preheat the oven to 375°. In a bowl, mix together the sugar and flour. Add the rhubarb and stir until evenly coated. Place in a greased 9 by 13-inch baking dish. In a separate bowl, combine the brown sugar and oats, and cut in the butter to make a crumbly topping. Sprinkle the topping over the rhubarb mixture. Bake for 40 minutes, until the rhubarb juice bubbles up through the golden brown topping. Serve warm with milk or cream.

These cookies get eaten faster than any others around here. When Leah lived at home, she fixed a lot of sugar cookies. My sugar cookie recipe makes a harder cookie than Leah's does, which Ben always teased me about. He would say, "Be sure you have your shoes on so the cookies don't fall on your toes." Ben was a joker and liked to tease, but he really liked my sugar cookies. This recipe is for soft sugar cookies, like Leah makes.

Soft Sugar Cookies

Makes 10 dozen

2 cups sugar

2 tablespoons baking powder

1 cup lard or shortening

1 tablespoon lemon juice

2 eggs

1/2 teaspoon vanilla extract

1 1/2 cups buttermilk or sour milk

1 tablespoon baking soda

1/4 teaspoon salt

4 to 5 cups all-purpose flour

Mix together the sugar, baking powder, lard, lemon juice, eggs, vanilla, buttermilk, baking soda, and salt in a large bowl. The mixture should be light in color and smooth and soft. Stir in enough of the flour to make a stiff dough; work it in with your hands. Chill the dough for a few hours or overnight.

Preheat the oven to 350°. Drop the dough by teaspoonfuls, 2 inches apart, onto lightly greased cookie sheets and bake for 10 to 12 minutes, until the edges are golden and crispy and the centers are soft to the touch. Allow the cookies to cool for 5 minutes before removing to wire racks to cool completely.

Storing cookies in a sealed container with a piece of bread inside will help keep the cookies moist and fresh for a long time.

The Amish Cook

by Elizabeth Coblentz

September 1997

I will try to write a quick column tonight. Paul Jr. seems to be doing great thus far. He turned two years old on Friday, August 22. That is the same birthday as our daughter Verena, who turned 31. We also have son Albert's daughter Elizabeth's birthday on the same date. Verena planned a taco supper for all the family and some others on her birthday. So our shed was cleaned out and everything was held in there. Was good to all be in one big room together. Then with everyone bringing some food, the big table was well filled.

On August 20, our sweet, loving granddaughter Mary (Paul Jr.'s sister) would've turned six years old. The final report of her death hasn't been fully announced. It must've been a sad time for the family when they spent some time at the grave of Mary on her birthday in the evening. Daughter Leah and children spent some of the day here, as it seemed such a hard day on them to think of Mary's birthday. It at times seems like a dream; we had Paul and Leah's four children with us for five weeks and four days while Paul Jr. was in the hospital.

Often, I think how their three oldest children went to school and Mary was here with me, my daughter Emma, and her baby, Elizabeth, during the day. She must've been lonesome at times, but surely never showed it. She often took care of little Elizabeth. She would often say to me, "Since I can't take care of Paul Jr., I can take care of Elizabeth," which she did. She was such a sweet little girl; I never had to scold her. So easy to care for her. Now that we think back she had such heavenly eyes. She was always such a little willing worker and took care of Paul Jr. while daughter Leah did her laundry. I often think back to when the undertaker brought Mary back home to be laid to rest. I put up her hair. It was so fluffy! The same hair I took care of for all those weeks. But I know God knew best for this Angel now in Heaven. How wonderful on her part!

Well I've got tomatoes, pickles, and hot peppers to can. Should pick them tomorrow. I am so glad for daughter Verena's help as she quit her job at the sewing factory after being there over thirteen years. She says she wants to help me with the work here at home and get work only a couple of days a week. So it is a change in this household now that Jacob and Emma have moved out and Verena is here during the day. Verena is good help.

Thursday we want to attend a quilting at one of my niece's. She has a quilt in frame to donate at the benefit auction on Saturday, September 14, for Paul and Leah. She told me to bring my girls along, so hopefully we can all go and get some completed for my niece.

Well it is bedtime; I need to hike off to bed where everyone else is resting peacefully.

Thank you to all those readers for the sympathy cards, encouraging letters, and money that has been sent to us. It has been so comforting to see all those readers with such encouraging letters. A hearty thank-you to you all.

Amish Oatmeal Bread

Makes 4 loaves

1 cup whole-wheat flour
2 cups quick-cooking oats
1/2 cup firmly packed brown sugar
2 tablespoons salt
4 tablespoons butter
4 cups boiling water
2 (1/4-ounce) packages active dry yeast
1 cup warm water
9 to 10 cups bread flour

In a large bowl, mix together the flour, oats, brown sugar, salt, and butter. Pour the boiling water over the top and mix. Let cool to lukewarm. Dissolve the yeast in the warm water and add to the oat mixture. Add enough bread flour to make an elastic dough and knead thoroughly until smooth. Place the dough in a large greased bowl and turn once so it's greased lightly on top. Cover with a loose piece of cheesecloth or plastic wrap and set in a warm, draft-free place to rise until double (about 2 hours).

Punch the dough down, then re-cover and let rise again until nearly double (about 90 minutes). Divide the dough evenly into 4 balls and shape into loaves. Place each loaf in a greased loaf pan, cover, and set in a warm, draft-free place to rise again until nearly double (about 90 minutes). Bake in a 350° oven for 30 minutes, until the loaves are nicely browned and sound hollow when tapped.

Snickerdoodles are an old favorite, brought to America by the Germans. No one is quite sure where the name comes from, although some think it could have come from two German words that sound similar to "snickerdoodle"—Schnecke, meaning "snail," or Snekrad, which is the snail-shaped part of a clock's insides (snickerdoodles have a snail shape). These cookies are nice and crisp on the outside and chewy on the inside. Like a lot of the foods brought to America on colonial ships, these cookies were made to last a long time without going stale. If you keep these tightly sealed, they'll taste good for weeks.

Snickerdoodles

Makes 2 1/2 dozen cookies

1 1/2 cups plus 1 tablespoon sugar

1 tablespoon ground cinnamon

1 cup shortening

2 eggs

1 teaspoon vanilla extract

2 3/4 cups all-purpose flour

1 teaspoon baking soda

1/2 teaspoon salt

2 teaspoons cream of tartar

Preheat the oven to 400°. Combine 1 tablespoon of the sugar and the cinnamon in a small bowl and set aside. Cream the shortening in a mixing bowl and gradually add the remaining sugar, beating well. Add the eggs and beat well. Stir in the vanilla. In a separate mixing bowl, combine the flour, baking soda, salt, and cream of tartar. Add this mixture to the sugar and eggs and beat well. Shape the dough into 1 1/2-inch balls, and roll each ball in the reserved sugar and cinnamon mixture. Place each ball 2 inches apart on a lightly greased cookie sheet. Bake for 8 minutes, until lightly browned. Allow the cookies to cool for 5 minutes before removing to wire racks to cool completely.

Chocolate chip cookies are favorites for passing out to the children before church and to the adults after church. These cookies are also Kevin's favorite. He always looks forward to munching on them during his visits. Sometimes my girls and Kevin will get into a snowball fight before he leaves. One time they stood in the driveway to block his car from leaving. Kevin didn't want to drive forward for fear of hitting them, so they just stood in front of his car. It was all in good fun. They say he is like a brother to them. And he eats these chocolate chip cookies just like a family member would. Ha!

Chocolate Chip Cookies

Makes 5 to 6 dozen large cookies

2 cups butter

2 cups granulated sugar

2 cups firmly packed brown sugar

4 eggs, beaten

2 teaspoons baking soda

2 teaspoons hot water

5 cups all-purpose flour

2 teaspoons salt

1 (12-ounce) package chocolate chips

2 teaspoons vanilla extract

Preheat the oven to 375°. Cream the butter and sugars together in a bowl until smooth. Add the eggs and mix well. In a small bowl, dissolve the baking soda in the hot water. Sift together the flour and salt. Add the baking soda liquid to the butter and sugar mixture alternately with the flour. Stir in the chocolate chips. Flavor with the vanilla. Drop the dough by teaspoonfuls, spaced 3 inches apart, onto greased cookie sheets. Bake for 10 to 12 minutes, until golden brown. Allow the cookies to cool for 5 minutes before removing to wire racks to cool completely.

After years of driving to Elizabeth's farm and unintentionally blinding the occupants of Amish buggies with my high beams, I tried to be considerate recently by turning off my lights completely as I passed. Instead of being helpful, I became the subject of gossip at the next Amish community church gathering, as folks anxiously discussed a dangerous stranger turning off his lights as he passed buggies.

These cookies have a good, sweet taste and are easy to make. We used to make molasses cookies all the time, but our tastes have changed and it just seems we make sugar or chocolate chip cookies most often these days. There used to be a cane mill in a nearby town, and when I was a teenager, my family raised cane and hauled it to the cane mill. There they made it into molasses. Pulling the cane and leaves from the stalks was hard work. I had cut marks on my hands for many years from pulling the cane. The cane mill is long gone, and the scars have slowly disappeared. Not many people around here grow sugar cane any more, but here is a recipe for using some of that yummy molasses.

Molasses Nut Cookies

Makes 10 dozen cookies

2 cups sugar

1 cup shortening

2 eggs, beaten

1 cup molasses

1 teaspoon vanilla extract

6 cups all-purpose flour

3 teaspoons baking soda

1 teaspoon salt

3 teaspoons ground cinnamon

2 teaspoons ground ginger

2 cups sour milk or buttermilk

1 cup chopped nuts

Preheat the oven to 375°. In a large bowl, cream together the sugar and shortening, then add the eggs, molasses, and vanilla and mix well. In a separate bowl, combine the flour, baking soda, salt, cinnamon, and ginger, and then add to the creamed mixture alternately with the sour milk. Stir in the nuts. Drop the batter onto greased cookie sheets by the teaspoonful, spaced 2 inches apart, and bake for 10 minutes, until golden around the edges. Allow the cookies to cool for 5 minutes before removing to wire racks to cool completely.

To cheer up older people, widows, and so on, a friend or relative anonymously sends gifts, money, and groceries, especially during holidays. The person receiving the gifts has fun trying to guess who their "secret pal" is all year long. The secret pal always passes the gifts through other families, so it's usually guess, guess, guess as to who it could be. At Christmas-time, the secret pal reveals him- or herself.

These cookies are common in Amish communities throughout northern Indiana. We used to make our own buttermilk as it could be used in so many different ways: in breads, muffins, biscuits, shortcakes. Buttermilk is also good for the skin, especially a baby's skin. And buttermilk baths can be used to soothe poison ivy irritations or chicken pox. But it's in baking that we use buttermilk the most. It's hard to keep these cookies around for very long, but they will keep for several days in a sealed cookie jar.

Buttermilk Cookies

Makes 3 dozen cookies

2 cups sugar

1 cup shortening

4 eggs

4 teaspoons vanilla extract

4 cups all-purpose flour

4 teaspoons baking powder

2 teaspoons baking soda

1 teaspoon salt

1 cup buttermilk

Preheat the oven to 425°. In a large bowl, cream together the sugar and shortening. Beat in the eggs, one at a time, then stir in the vanilla. Combine the flour, baking powder, baking soda, and salt in a separate bowl and then add to the creamed mixture alternately with the buttermilk. Drop by rounded teaspoonful, 2 inches apart, onto greased cookie sheets. Bake for 6 to 8 minutes. Allow the cookies to cool for 5 minutes before removing to wire racks to cool completely.

The Amish Cook

by Elizabeth Coblentz

October 1997

The largest benefit auction ever in these parts was held on Saturday, September 13, for Paul and Leah (my daughter) Shelter's two-year-old child, Paul Jr. The auction was to help pay hospital and medical bills resulting from Paul's heart surgeries over the summer.

Just the baked and canned goods brought in over $4,000. Phil Neuenschwander of Berne, Indiana, and twelve other area auctioneers donated their time. A hearty thank-you to all!

It started at 9:00 A.M. in the morning and sold all day till after 5:30 P.M., with two rings going on. Neuenschwander said this was the largest benefit auction he remembers ever held in the area. The number of items for sale totaled 980 with 266 buy numbers given out. Some of the high-priced items sold included a $900 hand-made quilt and a $1,300 grandfather clock. Even two candy suckers were auctioned off at $75. A 24-can case of Pepsi sold for $50.

A wide variety of donated items from livestock to homemade quilts, were auctioned off. Those attending the auction were not asked to pay a specific amount for their meal, but to donate whatever amount of money they chose. This helped raise more than

$9,000. There was 800 pounds of barbecued chicken, and the soups consisted of chicken-noodle, vegetable, and pot pie. Cole slaw, macaroni salad, and lettuce salad were also served along with ham sandwiches, hot dogs, pickles, catsup, mustard, and sliced tomatoes. There was also a root beer float stand and a lemonade stand. Coffee, pop, chips, and popcorn were also served. Plenty of food everywhere!

Neuenschwander, a well-known auctioneer in the area, has conducted fifteen benefit auctions for the Amish in his fifty-two years as an auctioneer, with this auction being the biggest in terms of profit. He has been inducted into the Reppert Auction Hall of Fame in Indiana. He graduated from Reppert Auctioneering School in 1945.

One of the unique aspects of Phil's auctioneering skills is that he can conduct auctions in both English and Swiss, which is the language of many of the Amish around here. So both Amish and non-Amish were able to participate in this auction. He did a wonderful job to take on this benefit auction for Paul and Leah's family.

It was so good to meet some of my readers of various places and to think one reader even brought a gift for me. Greatly appreciated. The auction day was so beautiful, couldn't have been nicer. And to top it all off, Paul Jr. seems to be doing better and better. Thanks to God!

It was an early start for a lot of us the morning of the auction. Baking was done all

day Friday, which was our family's way of helping to prepare for the auction. A lot of time was spent filling cups with Jell-O (seventeen boxes). Then Saturday morning was spent making Spaghetti and Meat Sauce (in 20-quart and 16-quart cookers), and making a big batch of potato salad really put us on the run—and the day had just begun.

So the food consisted of soups, crackers, salads, sandwiches, barbecued chicken, sliced tomatoes, home-baked bread buns, a variety of chips, Jell-O, ice cream, popcorn, coffee, pop, pickles, catsup, mustard, butter, apple butter, cake, and the beverage stands. Most all was donated, except for some items from the lunch stand. One item sold for donation was our one-horse mower, which sold for $500. We had a horse which pulled it so well and every Friday or Saturday I would mow our yard with it. It could get in close corners. That was around twenty-five years ago. I well remember one day when I was mowing the yard; daughter Leah was baking a birthday cake for my thirty-sixth birthday as to surprise me. Good old days are not forgotten. Leah was twelve years old at the time,

being thirteen the next Monday. She was so happy to surprise me with a cake. Wonderful old memories.

This is what I made for the benefit auction:

Spaghetti and Meat Sauce

Serves 60

25 pounds freshly ground beef
9 gallons tomato juice
6 pounds uncooked spaghetti
4 (32-ounce) jars spaghetti sauce
Salt
Pepper

Divide the ground beef between two 20-quart cookers. Cook until the beef is no longer pink, and then drain. Divide 4¹/2 gallons of the tomato juice between the two cookers, and let it come to a boil. Add 3 pounds of spaghetti to the boiling sauce in each cooker.

After the meat sauce again reaches a boil, let it cook for about 10 minutes, until the spaghetti is tender. Divide the remaining 4¹/2 gallons of tomato juice between the two cookers. Pour 2 jars of spaghetti sauce into each cooker. Sample the meat sauce and add salt and pepper to your taste. Allow the meat sauce to simmer for at least 20 minutes before serving so the flavors have time to blend.

Amish Language

Like most immigrants to the United States, the Amish brought their native language with them. Most immigrants have historically assimilated into the larger U.S. population, causing their native tongue to gradually die out after a generation or two. Because of their closed, isolated society, however, the Amish have managed to preserve their language. Today, most Amish are bilingual. They speak a Swiss or German dialect at home and use conversational English among outsiders. Most retain a German or Swiss accent even in their English speech.

Amish families that came directly, or almost directly, from Switzerland in the 1700s, still speak a mainly Swiss dialect. Today these families live primarily around Berne, Indiana, and Seymour, Missouri. Elizabeth comes from this lineage, speaking a Swiss dialect. Ben's family, like the majority of the Amish, spent a generation or two in Germany before coming to America. They speak a German dialect and comprise the large Amish populations of Pennsylvania, Ohio, and northern Indiana.

The evolution of Amish language parallels that of the French language spoken in Quebec, Canada. Separated from the mother country by generations and an ocean, the Canadian French language has absorbed many English words. These days, a Parisian might have difficulty understanding the French spoken in Quebec. Similarly,

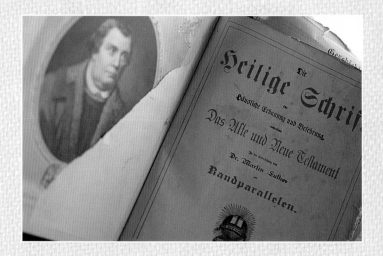

many English words have crept into the Swiss and German languages that the Amish speak, not to mention the effect regional accents have had. A Swiss or German native would also likely have difficulty understanding an Amish person.

My mother always spoke Swiss to us children, but when my dad and his brothers got together, they spoke English. I remember Mother and her sisters teasing them, asking if they didn't know how to speak Swiss. My dad and his two brothers married the three sisters of one family, which included Mother, naturally. When Ben first came to my parents' home, we spoke Swiss. He didn't understand it because he was raised in Ohio and New York speaking High German and English. His family moved to this area from Jamestown, New York, which is how we met.

Speaking two languages does come in handy sometimes. When our children were young and Ben and I didn't want them to know what we were saying, we'd speak in English. But too soon that ended, as they got in on the conversation. It was good that they knew the English language when they started school, though.

At home we still speak Swiss among ourselves. One day, however, we got a test of our Swiss. A couple traveling from Switzerland met some friends of ours. Our friends directed them here since they know we speak Swiss. It was so interesting to have them here. They enjoyed our Swiss yodels or anything that was sung in Swiss. We brought our Swiss language books out from our bookcase and they could really read them. We speak Swiss, but we have many English words in our Swiss language. Some of the Swiss words they spoke had to be said in English for us to understand.

When Ben and I were first married, tapioca was our main dessert. As times got better, I began to prepare other desserts. When I was growing up, tapioca was saved for when we had company. Tapioca can be cooked a couple of days ahead of time, then when company comes you have a good, quick, and delicious dessert ready to go. I like to let the tapioca set for a couple of hours before cooking it, and I always like to add fresh strawberries. If tapioca is stored in a cool place like a refrigerator, it will keep for a couple of days. You can also freeze it. If it is tightly sealed it will keep for quite awhile. Even today, with my beloved husband gone, I still enjoy a good dish of tapioca.

Homemade Tapioca Pudding

Serves 4 to 6

1/2 cup tapioca

2 cups water

3 tablespoons plus 1 1/2 teaspoons strawberry Jell-O (half of a 3-ounce box)

3/4 cups sugar

1 1/2 cups whipped cream

1/4 cup fresh strawberries, thinly sliced

In a 2-quart kettle, cook the tapioca and water over medium heat for 7 to 8 minutes, stirring often. Remove from the heat. The tapioca will be very thick and transparent. If the tapioca is too thick, add more water. Add the Jell-O and sugar and stir for 1 minute until well blended. Pour into a bowl to cool. Let set for 15 to 20 minutes at room temperature. Add the whipped cream and strawberries and mix well. The whipped cream will change the texture of the tapioca from elastic and stiff to very creamy. The pudding should be a deep pink color. Let cool in the refrigerator while setting, stirring occasionally.

Pie is often on the menu around here, although not as much as it used to be when my children were still living at home. Seems I was always making cherry, raisin, rhubarb-custard, pumpkin, and oatmeal pies back then.

One of the most important parts of a pie is the crust. The biggest mistake people make when fixing a pie crust is kneading the dough too much, which can make the crust hard. You don't have to worry about that with this recipe. You can roll and knead this never-fail pie dough as much as you want; this recipe always works. I was preparing for a wedding at my sister's years ago and some of the women had this never-fail recipe, and I have been using it ever since.

Never-Fail Pie Crust

Makes 2 (8-inch) pie crusts

2 cups all-purpose flour

3/4 teaspoon salt

2/3 cup lard or shortening

2 teaspoons apple cider vinegar

1 egg

3 1/2 tablespoons ice water

In a mixing bowl, combine the flour and salt. Cut in the lard with a pastry blender or two knives until the mixture is uniform (it should be fairly coarse). In a separate bowl, blend the vinegar, egg, and water. Make a well in the center of the flour mixture, pour the vinegar mixture into the well, and stir till blended. Work the dough into a ball. Divide this ball into two smaller balls. For each pie crust, press one ball into a flat circle with smooth edges. On a lightly floured surface, roll the dough to 1/8 inch thick with a diameter 1 1/2 inches larger than your pie pan. When rolling, work the dough from the center to the edge. Transfer the dough to the pie pan by lifting one edge of the dough onto the rolling pin and rolling the dough around the pin. Unroll the dough over the pie pan.

This is a common Pennsylvania German pie made from nonperishable ingredients, which made it practical for German and Swiss immigrants to take on the ships as they made their crossing from Europe to America in the 1800s. The story is that the pie was so sweet you had to shoo the flies away while it cooled.

I think all flies have to be on the shoo line of sweet pies. This pie uses molasses, which is popular in our community as a spread for our fried mush. I used to make Shoo-Fly Pie much more often, but it just doesn't go as fast as the berry pies.

Shoo-Fly Pie

Makes 1 (8-inch) pie

1 (8-inch) unbaked Never-Fail Pie Crust (see page 127)

1/3 cup molasses

1/4 cup boiling water

1/4 teaspoon baking soda

1 cup plus 3 tablespoons all-purpose flour

1/3 cup sugar

1/4 cup lard or shortening

Pinch of salt

Preheat the oven to 350°. Roll out the crust and line an 8-inch pie pan, as directed on page 127. Mix the molasses, water, and baking soda together in a small bowl and pour into the unbaked pie shell. In a separate bowl, combine the flour, sugar, lard, and salt and mix until crumbly. Place the flour mixture on top of the molasses mixture. Bake for 40 minutes, until the molasses mixture seeps through the top and the top is dark brown.

While the Amish are wary of modern medicine, natural and organic remedies are held in high esteem. Elizabeth and her daughters routinely seek out the services of a local Amish herb doctor who specializes in homeopathic cures. The relaxing foot massages they receive ease tension and soothe pains. A young Amish woman assists the doctor. One man relaxes so much during the foot treatment that he falls asleep. The Amish doctor works four days a week, and his services are sought out by Amish and non-Amish patients alike, as evidenced by his appointment calendar being booked solid for months.

This pie resembles a pecan pie in look, taste, and texture, but it has its own flavor. When my children were still at home, their favorite pies were cherry, raisin, and pumpkin. This oatmeal pie became a family favorite after we tasted it at a wedding.

I like to bake pies in glass pie pans. They look better that way and you can see how the crust is doing. This oatmeal pie is rich and easy to make. It keeps for days after being baked, and it seems that the longer it sits, the better it tastes.

Easy Oatmeal Pie

Makes 1 (8-inch) pie

1 (8-inch) unbaked Never-Fail Pie Crust (see page 127)

$^1/_2$ cup margarine or butter

$^3/_4$ cup firmly packed brown sugar

2 eggs

$^3/_4$ cup light corn syrup

$^3/_4$ cup rolled oats

$^1/_2$ cup walnut pieces

Preheat the oven to 350°. Roll out the crust and line an 8-inch pie pan, as directed on page 127. Melt the margarine in a small saucepan over low heat. In a mixing bowl, cream together the margarine, sugar, and eggs. Add the corn syrup, oats, and walnuts and mix. Pour into the pie shell and bake for 1 hour, until thickened inside and golden on top.

Rumspringa

Middlefield, Ohio, is a small Amish community about an hour's drive east of Cleveland. Amish women sell pies and homemade bread from the back of buggies, tour buses full of gawking curiosity seekers occasionally rumble through the streets, and banks have parking spaces as well as hitching posts to cater to their two very different clienteles.

One day I was munching on a sandwich in my car and savoring the peace of a Middlefield moment when I was suddenly jarred by the sound of rock music blaring from a battery-powered boom box. When I turned to search for the offending noise, I noticed that the boom box was sitting in the front seat of a horse-drawn buggy. The owner—a young, blonde Amish man—was sporting sunglasses, a half-unbuttoned shirt, and a lit cigarette. Shocked by what I thought was a blatant disregard for traditional Amish behavior, I told some Amish friends about my experience. They explained that I had witnessed a teenager in the throes of *Rumspringa*. No, it's not a deadly disease, it's a Pennsylvania German word that, roughly translated, means "running around period."

While most Amish children go through a fairly normal period of teenage restlessness, some go through a full-blown rebellion, or *Rumspringa*. During this time, Amish kids often smoke, drink, get their driver's license, attend wild parties, and wear non-Amish clothing. Because Amish aren't baptized until age twenty-one, teenagers aren't technically members of the church and therefore this behavior isn't a violation of the *Ordnung*. While Amish parents worry just as much as other parents, they generally turn a blind eye to the misbehavior, reasoning that if the children are allowed to explore the outside world and get everything out of their systems, they'll soon discover that the English world offers them very little. Considering that more than 90 percent of Amish children decide to remain in the Amish church as adults, the parents are usually right.

We don't grow our own cherries, although Ben and I tried. One year we put out a couple of cherry trees (one sweet, one sour), but they died out on us. Jacob put a peach tree in his yard, and he gets good, big peaches. I wouldn't mind having a peach tree.

Lovina's favorite pie is rhubarb-custard, Verena prefers cherry, and Amos and Albert enjoy bread pie. I like cherry or raisin pie. I add a little red food coloring to my cherry pie to make it look better. Also, I find that adding a little vinegar brings out the flavor in the cherries. That's just a tip that has been passed on to me down the line.

Cherry Pie

1 (8-inch) unbaked Never-Fail Pie Crust (see page 127)

2 cups home-canned cherries, or 4 cups store-bought canned and pitted cherries

3 tablespoons sugar

2 tablespoons Clear Jel (see hint)

1/2 teaspoon red food coloring

1/2 teaspoon apple cider vinegar

Preheat the oven to 400°. Roll out the crust and line an 8-inch pie pan, as directed on page 127. Mix the cherries, sugar, Clear Jel, red food coloring, and vinegar together in a saucepan. Cook over medium heat until thick. Pour into the pie shell and bake for 45 minutes, until the crust is brown.

Hint from Kevin: Clear Jel really makes this cherry pie taste superb. Although Elizabeth can buy Clear Jel at her local grocery store, you might have to order it through the mail. Try ordering through Kitchen Krafts at 800-776-0575 or Sweet Celebrations at 800-328-6722.

Rhubarb is common in most Amish gardens. It is easy to grow and can be used in many different recipes: shortcakes, crunches, coffeecakes, jams, breads, and pies, just to name a few. I've had rhubarb plants every year since I was married, and I usually put out about seven or eight rhubarb plants. I tried to grow rhubarb when we first moved here, but we had chickens at the time and they spoiled the plants. Now, my rhubarb grows well. It gives a lot of stalks, so you can just jerk the stalk off when it is ready and it will regrow.

This recipe gives you the tart taste of rhubarb with a sweet, cool custard. Although Mother used to make rhubarb custard with just milk, sugar, and flour, I prefer my recipe, which has a cornstarch thickening. It has a better taste this way.

Rhubarb-Custard Pie

Makes 1 (8-inch) pie

1 (8-inch) unbaked Never-Fail Pie Crust (see page 127)

3 cups diced fresh rhubarb

$1/2$ cup sugar

2 tablespoons cornstarch

$1/4$ teaspoon salt

1 egg

$3/4$ cup light corn syrup

1 tablespoon butter or margarine, softened

Preheat the oven to 450°. Roll out the crust and line an 8-inch pie pan, as directed on page 127. Place the rhubarb into the pie shell. In a bowl, combine the sugar, cornstarch, and salt. Add the egg and beat well. Add the corn syrup and butter. Beat well and pour over the rhubarb. Bake for 15 minutes. Decrease the heat to 350° and bake for 30 minutes more, until the rhubarb is tender.

The Amish Cook

by Elizabeth Coblentz

November 1997

Our fortieth wedding anniversary is now history for 1997. Ben and I celebrated our special day, October 17.

Lots of memories of all those bygone years. There were happy times, and, also, sad times. We are blessed with eight children (two sons and six daughters). We had twenty-three grandchildren, now twenty-two, since the death of granddaughter Mary, who is in such a better place.

All our family (a total of thirty-eight) went out for supper for our anniversary on Friday evening at a place called The East of Chicago Pizza Company, a celebration which was planned by the children. Also for our anniversary, daughter Leah had sewed eight pockets on a dishcloth and all eight children were to fill the pockets with money; we received a nice sum. She presented it to us while eating. The owner of the pizza place also gave us a fruit pizza for our fortieth anniversary. The evening was what you would call an enjoyable and relaxing one.

Yes, forty years ago, as I have written about before, was a time when Asian flu struck our area. It was a severe epidemic! My temperature went up to 105 degrees a week before our wedding. All our family came down with the flu except Ben, my dad, and sister. There were so many sick in the area at the time. Mother was still sick the Tuesday before our Thursday wedding. But an Amish lady came by with a home remedy called "tobacco salve" to rub into mother's chest. It took hold right away and she immediately recovered. I often wonder how the salve was made. You had to watch to not get the salve in the stomach area, only the chest.

Daughter Leah and her husband, Paul, had all our family invited for the following Sunday evening (October 19) for a barbecue supper, which every one of the family attended. So we all got together on Friday and Sunday evening. Paul Jr. seems to be really improving from open-heart surgery. He was two years old on August 22.

We had a light frost last night. Time of year to expect a killing frost. We still have vegetables and flowers to be taken from the garden. We made twenty-four jars of sauerkraut, a double batch of hot pepper butter, and sandwich spread the other day. Have more cabbage to make more sauerkraut.

A reader misplaced the recipe for hot pepper butter, so here it is again:

Hot Pepper Butter

Makes 7 pints

35 small (2 to 3 inches long) green chile peppers
5 small (2 to 3 inches long) red chile peppers
2 cups yellow prepared mustard
4 cups apple cider vinegar
6 cups sugar
1 tablespoon salt
1 cup all-purpose flour
1 1/2 cups water

Grind the peppers in a hand-grinder (or pulse in an electric food processor) until medium ground. Place in a large kettle and add the mustard, vinegar, sugar, and salt. Bring the mixture to a boil over medium heat and then decrease the heat to a simmer.

Combine the flour and water in a bowl to make a paste and stir into the pepper mixture. Bring to a boil once more over medium heat and cook for 5 minutes, stirring occasionally. Pour into sterilized pint jars and seal. Great on sandwiches!

CHAPTER 5

✳ ✳ ✳ ✳ ✳

Sundays and Special Occasions

There are many times throughout the year when the family gets together to celebrate and enjoy one another's company. Church services are held on a rotating basis every other Sunday in one of the church members' homes. Everyone ends up holding church about twice a year. When church is held at my place or at the home of someone in my immediate family, lots of time is spent beforehand preparing for the services. It's lots of work, but enjoyable to be working together with family. Hundreds of people might show up for the actual service, so it's a good time to meet with friends as well as family. Holy Communion services are only held twice a year. A foot-washing ceremony takes place at such an occasion, and church members take the Communion.

Of course, there are other times throughout the year that we celebrate special occasions. Our family Christmas gathering is held on January 1 every year. The family also gets together on Butchering Day, which usually happens in February. With the spring comes weddings; June is the most popular wedding month, but October is also gaining in popularity because of the nice weather and beautiful colors.

If someone has a child who turns twenty-one during the year, they'll have a surprise party, which is always a fun occasion. In our family, there are lots of birthdays in July. Also in July is a nearby town's annual Swiss heritage festival, which is another occasion to meet with friends. And every four years during the summer there is a reunion of scribes sponsored by **The Budget** (see page 90) in Sugarcreek, Ohio. The last reunion I attended was with Ben in 1996.

As autumn arrives, the children sometimes put on special programs at school, and quilting bees are held by women in the community. Sometimes our family gets together in the fall to process the freshly fallen apples into applesauce and cider. There is always lots of canning to do in the fall too, which brings everyone together, and those who still farm sometimes hold a corn-husking bee at the time of harvest. Thanksgiving brings families together also, with a giant stuffed turkey and plenty of other food.

Before you know it, it's time for the family Christmas gathering again! Sundays and special occasions are always good times for food and fellowship with family and friends.

The Amish Cook

by Elizabeth Coblentz

July 1998

July Fourth was well spent around here. The evening before, five tents were set up in our yard for our visiting children to camp out. Daughter Liz and husband Levi cooked a ham bone and beans on the open fire in an iron kettle. Made one think of years ago when we used to cook potatoes (in their jackets) like that. Cooking outside kept the heat out of the house. Well, our fun evening outside ended when a storm came up during the night so everyone took for the house. Twenty-seven in all for lodging for the night was somewhat different, but enjoyable for a holiday. Coming in the kitchen it looked like a lot of dishes, but being stormy outside, and us all together, the women washed all those messy containers until 2:00 A.M.

The next morning, the morning of July 4, daughter Liz and husband Levi were once again the chief cooks. They made a fire with brick blocks with racks placed on top; eggs, potatoes, toast, bacon, and sausage gravy all made for a delicious breakfast. It looked so neat. Folding tables and benches were set up in the yard and all twenty-seven ate out in the open. I baked forty biscuits and also made a white gravy in the house. There were quite a few other goodies along with the morning meal.

As everyone left we had happy memories of July Fourth even with the rain out of the camp-out. After breakfast, a water battle took place, which our children enjoy (splashing, spraying with water). On the Fourth of July evening, we enjoyed an evening meal at the dairy farm where my husband works.

Well, I had best get dinner on the table as I have plenty to do, seventy to eighty people here for supper tonight.

Thank you for the birthday cards from you readers.

Must hurry. Made some cottage cheese recently. If you have sour milk, heat it till hot, not boiling. Remove from heat. Let cool. Then strain and add salt and pepper to your taste and add some milk or cream. Chill for a while before eating. Surprisingly, so many who have tasted this cottage cheese say that they prefer it.

Here's a recipe for some good brownies that freeze well.

Zucchini Brownies

Makes 2 dozen brownies

4 eggs
1 1/2 cups vegetable oil
2 cups sugar
2 cups all-purpose flour
2 teaspoons baking soda
2 teaspoons ground cinnamon
1 teaspoon salt
1/4 cup unsweetened cocoa powder
1 teaspoon vanilla extract
3 cups shredded zucchini
1 cup chopped walnuts or pecans

Preheat the oven to 350°. Combine the eggs, oil, and sugar in a large bowl. In a separate bowl, sift together the flour, baking soda, cinnamon, salt, and cocoa. Slowly add the flour mixture to the sugar mixture. Add the vanilla, zucchini, and nuts to the batter and mix thoroughly; batter will be very thick. Spread into a 15 by 10-inch jelly-roll pan. Bake for 30 minutes, until the center is set. Frost cool brownies with Vanilla Frosting (see page 170).

Homemade potato salad is a staple of special occasions. We don't eat it for meals at home, but we often have potato salad for picnics, at barn raisings, at after-church dinners, and for wedding suppers. Everyone seems to have their own family recipe that is slightly different from everyone else's. I got my potato salad recipe from my mother. It's a good hearty salad.

Amish Potato Salad

Serves 4 to 6

3 hard-boiled eggs, cooled

3 cups cooked, diced, and chilled potatoes with skins on

$3/4$ cup Salad Dressing (see page 167) or Miracle Whip

$1 1/2$ teaspoons yellow prepared mustard

2 tablespoons apple cider vinegar

$1/4$ small onion, chopped fine

$3/4$ cup sugar

1 teaspoon salt

$1/2$ cup chopped celery

2 tablespoons milk

Peel the eggs and mash them with a potato masher in a large bowl. Add the potato, salad dressing, mustard, vinegar, onion, sugar, salt, celery, and milk and mix well. The salad will be moist.

Hint: More celery can be added if your taste prefers it. This salad will keep in the refrigerator for several days.

This is a fun meal to have for a birthday celebration, as everyone can participate in making it. It is a layered dish where all the ingredients you prefer are piled up. This makes a quick meal in the summertime when we have a plentiful supply of lettuce from the garden. Haystacks are also popular at the Sunday evening gatherings of young people.

Haystack Supper

2 pounds freshly ground beef

1 (1¹/4-ounce) package taco seasoning

1 pound spaghetti

1 cup milk

1 pound American or Cheddar cheese, grated

¹/2 pound saltine crackers, crushed

1 head iceberg lettuce, chopped

2 onions, diced

4 tomatoes, diced

2 cups diced red or green bell peppers

Cook the ground beef in a skillet. Add the taco seasoning and stir until well combined. Remove from the heat and set aside. Boil the spaghetti in a kettle of water until soft. Drain the water and set the noodles aside. In a 3-quart saucepan over low heat, gradually add the milk to the cheese to make a thin sauce. Keep the sauce warm, but don't burn it.

Place the ground beef, spaghetti, crackers, lettuce, onion, tomato, and peppers in separate bowls on the table. On individual plates, layer the ingredients in this order: crackers, ground beef, lettuce, spaghetti, onion, tomato, and peppers. Then cover with the cheese sauce and serve right away.

Birthday Suppers

Birthdays are a happy occasion in this household. With such a large family it is not unusual for birthdays to fall on the same day. Ben's birthday, February 17, is on the same day as my brother-in-law's, so we used to get together for a special double celebration. We'd switch whose house we celebrated that occasion in each year.

Perhaps one of the biggest birthdays celebrated is the twenty-first birthday. That's the age of adulthood and everyone gets a surprise party. Often the surprise party is held several months before the actual birthday, making it a real

surprise. Such a surprise party might consist of telling the birthday boy or girl that they need to run an errand in town. When they get back, the house is full of food and friends. With our daughter Leah, all the young people were hiding in the washhouse. Verena's surprise party was also typical. I took her to town toward the evening and tried to waste time as the young people gathered at our house at a prearranged time. When Verena and I arrived home, everyone popped out from behind the washhouse and hollered out, "Surprise!" If a family doesn't wish to have a surprise party, they'll just have a dinner. We had surprise parties for all of our children when they turned twenty-one. They all got a good surprise.

"Over the river and through the woods to Grandfather's house we go. The horse knows the way to carry the sleigh over the white and drifted snow." Poems such as this make the good old days sound like happier, easier times. But would we really want to go back to them? I am thankful on Thanksgiving Day when I think of the struggles the Pilgrims must've gone through. We shall never know the terrors they braved all those years ago. We should be thankful for the bounteous harvest, and for so many things, but too often we forget.

Lots of gatherings and weddings occur on Thanksgiving Day. On that day the menu is turkey, stuffed chicken, sweet potatoes, pumpkin pie, cranberry salad, and pumpkin bread or rolls. Sometimes we have chicken, and other times we have a farm-raised turkey, but the one thing our table is never without on Thanksgiving Day is a good sweet potato casserole. It's tradition in our family.

Thanksgiving Sweet Potato Casserole
Serves 6

6 dark-skinned sweet potatoes, peeled

3 eggs

1 cup sugar

$1/4$ cup butter

1 cup milk

1 cup raisins

1 teaspoon ground cinnamon

$1/2$ cup chopped nuts

1 ($10 1/2$-ounce) package miniature marshmallows

Preheat the oven to 350°. Boil the sweet potatoes until tender in a pot of boiling water to cover. Drain and mash until creamy. Add the eggs, sugar, butter, milk, raisins, cinnamon, and nuts and mix well. Pour into a baking dish and cover with the marsh-mallows. Bake for 30 minutes, until lightly browned on top. Serve hot.

One year we had a huge winter storm. The roads were drifted in snow so there was no traffic. It was our evening to have my brother-in-law Emanuel's family and all their married children here to celebrate Ben and Emanuel's birthdays. As I was sewing and cleaning that day our children kept saying, "I wonder if they will show up for supper?" I thought, no way, as they couldn't come down our drifted road. Well, lo and behold, an hour before they were supposed to arrive our road was plowed through for one-lane traffic by the county. And, sure enough, the family showed up. The women pitched in and we soon had a good meal prepared. We always have a laugh on this evening, thinking of that snowy night. We had plenty of food and an enjoyable time together eating this hearty potato casserole.

Potluck Potato Casserole

Serves 4 to 6

2 pounds jacketed-boiled potatoes, chopped

3/4 cup melted butter

1 teaspoon salt

1/4 teaspoon pepper

1/2 cup chopped onion

2 cups Cream of Chicken Soup (see page 168), or 1 (10 3/4-ounce) can condensed cream of chicken soup plus 1 can water

2 cups whipping cream

2 cups grated sharp Cheddar cheese

2 cups corn flakes, crushed

Preheat the oven to 350°. Combine the potatoes with 1/2 cup of the melted butter in a large mixing bowl. Add the salt, pepper, onion, soup, cream, and cheese. Blend thoroughly. The mixture will be rather soupy, but it thickens rather quickly after cooking begins. Pour into a greased 5-quart casserole dish. In a small bowl, combine the corn flakes and the remaining 1/4 cup of melted butter. Sprinkle over the top of the mixture and bake for about 60 minutes, until the top is golden.

On Sunday evenings the young folks gather in the house or a well cleaned-out shed. Tables and benches are set up so the kids can sing together from the church songbook, which is called the *Ausbund*. After quite a few church songs are sung, they sing other songs and yodel. Then they might play a ring game like Farmer in the Dell, Chinese checkers, or volleyball by lantern light on the lawn. It's an evening of good, wholesome fun. About 10:30 or 11:00 P.M., most are ready to leave for home. That's when a boy and girl who might be interested in going steady will meet up. The boy will take the girl home on his horse-drawn buggy. If they go steady long enough, marriage will be on the list. A good meatloaf can be served at such a gathering.

Meatloaf

Serves 6

1 1/2 pounds freshly ground beef

1 cup quick-cooking rolled oats

1/2 cup chopped onion

1 teaspoon salt

2 teaspoons pepper

4 eggs, beaten

1/3 cup catsup

2 tablespoons firmly packed brown sugar

1 tablespoon yellow prepared mustard

Preheat the oven to 350°. Combine the ground beef, oats, onion, salt, pepper, and eggs in a bowl and mix thoroughly. Pack firmly into a 7 by 11-inch pan. In a small bowl, combine the catsup, brown sugar, and mustard, and pour over the meatloaf. Bake for 1 hour and 15 minutes, until the sauce has deepened in color and appears dry, and cracks have formed on top of the meatloaf. Let stand for 5 minutes before slicing.

When I was visiting Elizabeth recently, she was lamenting over what to get her thirty-plus grandchildren for Christmas. Her dilemma pales in comparison to what her own grandparents faced with more than one hundred grandchildren. In those days, the grandparents gave each child a bag filled with candy and perhaps a small dish or handkerchief—simple tokens that have become priceless treasures with time.

The Amish Cook

by Elizabeth Coblentz

December 1998

This is Christmas week, and it brings back memories of when all eight of our children were still in our care. Life was very busy then with washing, ironing, sewing, and cleaning. It was definitely a hustle and bustle at that time. I recall sewing at the sewing machine till late at night while our little peaceful sleepers were in bed. That's the quiet time when I made headway with finishing their new clothes to be given to them as Christmas gifts. My eyes couldn't take it now to sew by the light of the kerosene lamp. Now we have six children married and twenty-five grandchildren to think of (we had twenty-six, but the good Lord took Mary into His care). Glad I have two hard-working girls, Susan and Verena, at home yet to help out.

When the children were in our care, on Christmas Eve we put eight plates on our dining room table later in the evening when the little ones had fallen asleep. We filled the plates with candy and peanuts and put their gifts beside each plate. We always gave a glass dish with each plate as a remembrance in years to come. All kinds of games and toys were always enjoyed the next morning when Santa had come down the chimney. Ha! Those were the good old days.

I feel the children all took good care of what they got at Christmas. I'd always liked to sew new clothes for all the family: same color and material. I hardly do much baking and candy-making like I did back then. I always baked a lot of cookies and made various kinds of candy (peanut butter cups were a favorite). They didn't last long around here then. Fruitcakes were also made.

Breakfast was had in the morning, and some candy, but eating candy in the morning isn't the best idea. We also peeled oranges and ate them. We never decorate for Christmas as our electricity always runs out. Ha!

There weren't as big of gifts years ago; there just wasn't the money. But the children were just as happy. Money wasn't as plentiful, but what is the true meaning of Christmas? It's not money.

We always took the young ones to town before Christmas to see Santa. They were so glad for their sack of candy from Santa and telling him what they wanted for Christmas.

It's good to see our grandchildren today wear the clothes I made as our youngest daughter outgrew them. It is a real help to these young mothers to have them. It's good to have plenty of good Sunday clothes and school clothes.

We are having our Christmas gathering on New Year's Day of 1999 with our six married children and families all over for the day. There will be forty-one in all. They'll come for breakfast; they look forward to mother and grandmother's breakfast. Everyone will also be seated to eat at dinnertime. There will also be plenty of snacks in the afternoon, and for whoever is still hungry, there will be an evening meal. Gifts are passed out to everyone. We've started this New Year's Day tradition going since the children started to be married. The New Year's Song is sung in German along with Christmas carols several times during the day. This is a tradition passed down from my grandparents to my parents.

Our first snow of the season appeared here on December 16. This is the first time in all my years that I can recall a first snow this late. Good thing we can't rule the weather. God is above all, regardless.

Here is a recipe for the peanut butter cup candy I used to make:

Peanut Butter Cups

Makes about 5 dozen

1 pound peanut butter
1 cup margarine or butter
1 1/2 pounds powdered sugar
1 (6-ounce) package semisweet chocolate
*   chips, melted*

In a bowl, mix together the peanut butter and margarine and then work in the powdered sugar. Shape into balls the size of big marbles. Dip in the melted chocolate and let set on a wax paper–covered cookie sheet until cool. Delicious!

Sunday evenings are a special time for the young people in our community. At age sixteen and older, the young folks get together for singing and sometimes an evening meal. Tables and benches are set up and the food is prepared by the parents. After supper, the young people play volleyball and other ball games out in a field. Others might play horseshoes. Some of the girls will help with the dishes, so it's not so much work for the parents. One of the favorite Sunday night dishes among the young people is a good homemade pizza.

Homemade Pizza

Makes 1 pizza

1 uncooked Homemade Pizza Dough
(see page 169)

$1/2$ quart home-canned chunk beef,
or $1/2$ pound freshly ground beef

1 cup Mother's Pizza Sauce
(see page 169) or store-bought
pizza sauce

$1/2$ ($10\,3/4$-ounce) can condensed cream
of mushroom soup

$1/2$ pound Colby cheese, grated

Preheat the oven to 450°. Roll out the dough and line a pizza pan or baking sheet, as directed on page 169. Fry the beef until browned and drain well. Before adding the ingredients to the pizza crust, pop the dough in the oven for 3 minutes. This will make spreading the sauce easier. Spread the pizza sauce over the crust and top with the beef. Then drop the mushroom soup by teaspoonfuls evenly on top of the beef. (The mushroom soup will spread while baking.) Sprinkle the cheese on top and bake for 25 minutes, until the edges are brown.

Hint: Some people might prefer less beef and more cheese.

If a boy is interested in going steady with a young girl, he will ask to take her home. And this will begin a weekly pattern of "seeing each other" at Sunday evening singings. As the courtship progresses, they will begin to exchange letters and cards through the mail, and see each other through the week, sometimes for dinner with the family. Sometimes the courtship process can last for many years. Most Amish men and women marry by their mid-twenties.

Can you make something out of nothing? I'm not sure about the answer to that, but I do know how to make Nothings out of something. Kevin had been a regular visitor to our home for a year before he heard about Nothings. That's because Nothings are reserved for weddings. In 1992, a year after we first met Kevin, we were preparing for the wedding of our daughter Liz. I remember telling him that we had to prepare "nothings." We got a laugh when he said, "Elizabeth, you can't make nothing, you're going to have a thousand people show up for dinner."

Nothings, a traditional wedding pastry, are round and concave and sometimes sprinkled with powdered sugar. They are stacked on the wedding table (the table adorned with the wedding cake) so the pastry does double-duty as a treat and a decoration. I am not sure how these desserts got the name Nothings—we've just always called them that. In other Amish communities, these pastries are called "knee patches." The origins of this differently named dessert are a mystery to me. No Amish wedding in this part of Indiana would be complete without the batches of Nothings.

Amish Wedding Nothings

Makes 7 Nothings

1 egg

3/4 cup cream

Pinch of salt

2 to 3 cups all-purpose flour

Vegetable shortening or lard for deep-frying

Powdered sugar for sprinkling

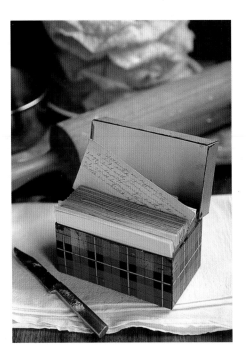

Beat the egg and stir in the cream, salt, and enough flour to make a stiff, elastic dough. Divide the dough into six or seven balls and roll each ball flat and very thin (1/16 inch). Cut three 2-inch slits, one above the other, through the middle of each piece.

Heat the shortening in a large kettle over high heat. When the shortening reaches 365°, or a piece of dough tossed in sizzles, put one piece of dough at a time into the kettle. Turn each piece over with two forks when you see a slight golden color. Take out and put on a plate covered with paper towels to drain. Sprinkle powdered sugar over the top. Stack all of the Nothings on one plate and serve.

Wedding Dinner

There are many duties to attend to before a wedding day. Although weddings are announced in church only about two weeks before the ceremony, the immediate family knows about a month ahead of time. They will quietly begin to make preparations like starting on a big batch of homemade noodles. If someone spots a group of women making noodles, they'll half jokingly inquire, "Is there a wedding coming up?"

Weddings are usually held on a Thursday, so the Saturday before, some of the furniture from the house is carried somewhere to be stored, and some is rearranged. The inside of the home needs to be completely redone to accommodate the large wedding crowd. Some couples have their wedding tables set up in a cleaned-out shed, which is easier because no furniture has to be moved from inside the house. When the ceremony is held in a house, folding tables will be set up with benches to seat the people. We have held four weddings in our home for our daughters. We have two sheds on our property, so one was used for cooking the meals and for additional seating, and the other was used for the actual service where the couple was united in marriage.

Usually the wedding cakes are baked by the immediate family on the Saturday or Monday before the wedding. A variety of cakes, perhaps twenty-five to thirty, are frosted after they are baked and cooled. At my wedding we had chocolate, white, and spice cakes. The main wedding cake for all of our daughters had four layers, each about 5 inches thick, so it was a good-sized cake. It was nicely frosted and decorated with coconut and tiny silver ball candies. There are also what you call "side cakes" with "Good Luck" and "Best Wishes" written on them. The two side cakes are set on either side of the wedding cake in the couple's "wedding corner." The wedding corner is a corner of the room where the married couple and their attendants are seated for dinner. The corner dishes are always kept separate from the other dishes when they're being washed. These dishes, which are usually a gift to the bride from the groom, will be saved for a special remembrance.

The Tuesday before the wedding, twenty or more women, usually immediate family and friends, come to bake the pies. Raisin, cherry, oatmeal, pumpkin, and rhubarb are popular pies at weddings around here. We usually have at least three or four varieties of pies. The women also make the Nothings, and toast the breadcrumbs for dressing. Amish Wedding Nothings, a traditional wedding pastry, is deep-fried dough cooked till golden brown and sprinkled with powdered sugar. The pastries are tasty, but they are also decorative. The edges of the Nothings curl up after being deep-fried so they can be stacked on top of each other on plates and placed on the wedding tables. We usually make sixty to ninety pies and thirteen to fifteen batches of Nothings.

Twelve or more single girls assist us on the Wednesday before the wedding. They peel potatoes (four or five 20-quart cookers full), make the colorful carrot salad, help set the remaining tables, and do whatever has to be done. In this part of Indiana, celery stalks are placed upright in simple white vases to make a centerpiece for each table. Lately, the women and the single girls have started making all of their

(continued)

preparations together on Wednesday. I like it this way as everything gets done in one day and the pies are fresher.

The bride and groom have two couples for their attendants and have ten to fifteen unmarried couples to wait on the tables. When Ben and I got married we had seven couples for table waiters. Couples usually have many more these days.

The table waiter girls wear a light blue dress and white cap and apron. The brides in different Amish communities wear different colored dresses. In some conservative Indiana settlements, the Amish brides wear a black dress with a white cap and apron. Amish women are traditionally buried in the same dress they are married in. Amish men typically wear a tie at their wedding, along with a black suit and white shirt. It's the only time in his life that an Amish man wears a tie.

Rings are part of the Amish wedding, but not in the same way as our English counterparts. A ring is stuck in the wedding cake. When the cake is cut in the evening to pass around to the young people and the family, someone usually finds the ring in their cake, and it's theirs to keep.

On the day of the wedding, I usually ask thirty women to help with the cooking. Here's a list of the food we had for our oldest daughter's wedding. It was our first try and it seemed an impossible task to gather all the ingredients for this meal.

* 250 pounds of fried chicken
* 40 quarts of chicken and noodles
* 20 quarts of mashed potatoes
* 16 quarts of homemade gravy
* Dressing (made in three 13-quart dishpans)
* 5 gallons of pork and beans
* 25 gallons of carrot salad (made with 42 boxes of orange Jell-O)
* 8 gallons of potato salad
* 12 heads of lettuce for salad
* 8 gallons of 24-hour coleslaw
* 150 pounds of boneless ham
* Home-canned fruit salad
* Homemade pickles
* Home-canned buttered corn
* 30 pounds of cheese
* 16 bunches of celery
* 900 cookies
* 33 cakes
* 88 pies (cherry, raisin, and pumpkin)
* 15 batches of Nothings
* 10 pounds of tapioca pudding served with 12 cans of Rich's topping

*On Sunday church evenings I often won-
der who will arrive for the meal. I remember one Sunday when 179 people came for
supper! If I'd known we'd have that many
I would've made more baked goods and
desserts, but I think we did well with
what we had. We peeled and mashed
potatoes, fixed lots of chicken and noodles, brought out the home-canned food
in our basement, and kept going out to
the garden to pick more lettuce. As people
kept coming, we kept cooking. It was one
church evening I will never forget. This
chicken casserole is a good one to serve to
a large group of people.*

Company Chicken Casserole

Serves 8 to 10

4 cups diced carrots

4 quarts diced potatoes

2 cups diced celery

1 large onion, diced

8 cups frozen peas

4 to 5 quarts cooked boneless
chicken pieces

1 teaspoon salt

1 teaspoon pepper

1 cup grated Colby cheese

Preheat the oven to 350°. Place the carrots,
potatoes, celery, onion, and peas in a kettle
with water to cover. Bring to a boil over
medium-high heat, then decrease heat to
medium and cook for 20 minutes, until the
vegetables are tender. Drain the vegetables
and place in a large roaster with a lid. Add the
chicken and mix well. Add salt and pepper.
Sprinkle the cheese on top and cover the
roaster with its lid. Cook for 1 hour, until the
cheese is melted.

Some Amish communities refer to this pie as "funeral pie" because it is commonly served at funeral gatherings. We have never called it that, however. Around here, Raisin Pie is often served at weddings. We just buy our raisins from the store. This pie will keep for several days.

Raisin Pie

2 (8-inch) unbaked Never-Fail Pie Crusts (see page 127)

1 cup raisins

2 tablespoons clear gelatin

Pinch of salt

1 cup sugar

1 tablespoon apple cider vinegar

1 cup water

Preheat the oven to 400°. Roll out the crusts and use one to line an 8-inch pie pan, as directed on page 127. Cook the raisins with water to cover in a kettle over medium heat until plump and juicy, about 15 to 30 minutes. In a bowl, make a thickening with the gelatin, salt, sugar, vinegar, and water. Pour into the raisin mixture. Cook until the mixture is thick enough to stick to a spoon. Add more sugar if it is not sweet enough for you. Pour into the pie shell. Cover the top with the remaining pie shell and seal and flute the edges. Cut slits in the center for steam to escape. Bake for 30 minutes, until the top is golden brown.

Hint: A lattice-top pie crust can also be used.

Some desserts are saved for certain occasions, like a quilting bee. I have been to many quilting bees. These are occasions when thirty to forty women from a community gather to make one, two, or even three quilts in a day. The women gather around the frame and the stitching (and the gossip) begins! I often wonder how many stitches are in a quilt. The bee begins around 7:00 A.M., with coffee and snacks like pastries and cookies served in the forenoon. A good noon meal of mashed potatoes, vegetables, and salad is also served to all who attend. A lot of yodeling and singing and gossiping goes on at a quilting bee.

The Amish Cook

by Elizabeth Coblentz

October 1999

It is a crisp 33 degrees this beautiful morning, and I must get this written. There's always plenty to do, it seems. Maybe it would be best to take a break from some of this work soon to visit our aged or shut-in neighbors. Good health means so much.

This year has been stressful with health problems in the family, but there is also so much to be thankful for. God, the One who makes no mistakes, has a purpose for it all.

Our crops are all harvested now, crops of corn and soybeans out of our fields. Our neighbor has farmed for us since 1958. The years have a way of slipping by. Wonder what the winter will hold. Will it be cold and snowy? With plenty of snow, our horse-drawn sleighs can be used. Being snowbound too long isn't my favorite thing. I often wonder what the year 2000 holds. God only knows.

Sewing has been our focus the past couple of weeks. As all our clothing is made by hand, it takes a lot of time. My daughter Lovina, her children, Emma, and her daughter spent the day here yesterday. Our sewing machines were in gear. The last two weeks, they've made two dresses and aprons for Susan and one outfit, almost completed, for me. Also, they have made six children's dresses and aprons, and Emma tried her luck with cutting out and sewing a coat. Emma used to work at a sewing factory, so she knows how to put it all together. I am so glad this sewing is getting done. Two men's shirts were also made.

While Lovina and Emma have been at the sewing machines working, I usually am in the kitchen preparing meals, washing dishes, and canning. It has been wonderful to spend all this time together.

Well, I must eat some breakfast. Verena has prepared it, and it smells so good. Susan is doing the sweeping. Susan has been unable to work since the tri-break of her ankle May 16, and then an infection set in. Hopefully it will heal completely soon. We just try to take one day at a time.

I continue to harvest late-season goodies from the garden. Turnips and radishes are continuing to go good. A reader in Jacksonville, NC, sent me some turnip seeds earlier this season. They are coming up nicely. A hearty thank-you to people who have sent seeds. There are also a few pumpkins that need to be harvested.

This recipe for Whoopie Pies is a favorite among the children. It got its name from the way the children would react when they found one in their dinner buckets—"whoopie!"

Whoopie Pies

Makes 2 dozen Whoopie Pies

Cookies

4 cups all-purpose flour
1 cup unsweetened cocoa powder
2 teaspoons baking soda
1/8 teaspoon salt
1 cup lard or shortening
2 cups sugar
2 eggs
2 teaspoons vanilla extract
1 tablespoon apple cider vinegar
1 cup less 1 tablespoon milk
1 cup hot water

Filling

3 tablespoons all-purpose flour
1 cup milk
3/4 cup lard or shortening
1 1/2 cups powdered sugar
2 teaspoons vanilla extract

Preheat the oven to 350°. To make the cookies, in a bowl, sift together the flour, cocoa, baking soda, and salt. In a separate bowl, cream the lard, sugar, eggs, and vanilla until smooth. Pour the vinegar in a 1-cup measure and then add the milk to sour. Add the dry ingredients and the sour milk alternately to the egg mixture, blending well. Add the hot water and blend until smooth. Drop by teaspoonfuls, spaced apart, onto cookie sheets. Bake for 8 minutes, until golden brown and crispy around the edges. Allow the cookies to cool for 5 minutes before removing to wire racks to cool completely.

To make the filling, place the flour in a saucepan. Using a whisk, gradually add the milk and whip until smooth. Cook over medium-high heat for 5 to 7 minutes, stirring constantly, until thick. Remove from the heat. Cover and refrigerate until completely cool. In a mixing bowl, cream together the lard, sugar, and vanilla. Add the cooled milk mixture and beat for 7 minutes, until fluffy.

To assemble the Whoopie Pies, spread the filling on the bottom side of 12 cookies. Top the filling with the remaining 12 cookies, bottom-side down, to make a cookie "sandwich."

Hint: Some folks wrap the Whoopie Pies individually in foil then freeze them. We like to eat them at room temperature, but they taste good frozen too.

In the winter, when it's cold outside, a homemade cake will last ten days. In the summer, it might mold after a week. In families like ours, there usually isn't any cake left over after that long anyway. You really have to watch cakes left over from spring and summer weddings. Some people freeze their cakes after the wedding. Salad dressing cakes are often fixed for a birthday party. It's an easy one to make when you want to fix a cake from scratch. We never bought cake mixes when I was a girl; we always made white cake, chocolate cake, and spice cake from scratch. I liked chocolate cake the best. Amos and Albert liked to eat their cake with milk. They would pour a cup of milk over their cake in a bowl and eat it. This Salad Dressing Cake is a favorite here because it's easy to fix and full of chocolate. It's a good, moist cake.

Salad Dressing Cake

Makes 1 (8-inch) double-layer cake

2 cups all-purpose flour

2 teaspoons baking soda

5 tablespoons unsweetened cocoa powder

1 cup sugar

1 cup Salad Dressing (see page 167) or Miracle Whip

1 cup water

1 teaspoon vanilla extract

Preheat the oven to 350°. In a mixing bowl, sift together the flour, baking soda, and cocoa. Add the sugar, salad dressing, water, and vanilla and mix very well. Pour the batter into two greased 8-inch layer pans. Bake for 45 minutes, or until a toothpick inserted into the center comes out clean. Frost with Quick Caramel Frosting (see page 170).

We make cakes often around here, especially for a birthday party or as a carry-in dish. Sometimes food has to be carried from place to place, like for a large gathering. Sturdy food that can be stored in the wood buggy box during the ride works best. Once Amos, Albert, and Liz were riding to church in a homemade sleigh (with skids) on the snow-covered roads. As they turned the corner onto a different road, the cake they were taking to church came sliding out from under the seat and onto the road. It landed perfectly and did not ruin the cake! This chocolate cake recipe was my favorite growing up and is a good dessert to bring to a church gathering or a birthday party.

Chocolate Cake

Makes 1 (9 by 13-inch rectangular) cake

1 cup lard or shortening

2 cups sugar

2 eggs, beaten

8 tablespoons unsweetened cocoa powder

2 cups milk

2 tablespoons lemon juice or apple cider vinegar

2 cups all-purpose flour

Pinch of salt

2 teaspoons baking soda

1 teaspoon vanilla extract

Preheat the oven to 350°. Cream together the lard, sugar, eggs, and cocoa in a bowl. In a separate bowl, combine the milk and lemon juice and let set for at least 5 minutes. Add this to the creamed mixture. Mix in the flour, salt, baking soda, and vanilla. The batter will be thin. Pour into a greased 9 by 13-inch pan and bake for about 1 hour, until a toothpick inserted into the center comes out clean. Frost with Quick Caramel Frosting (see page 170).

Hint: When souring the milk with the lemon juice, be sure to let it set for at least 5 minutes before adding it to the batter. If the milk is not sour enough, the cake will go flat.

Holidays are special times around here. When our children were still living at home, we'd set the table for a special morning breakfast after they went to bed. All the plates on the table would be filled with candy and gifts for when our children awoke Christmas morning. Everyone always woke up early. The tradition in our family is for everyone—the whole extended family—to get together on New Year's Day. With everyone having their own families and commitments on Christmas Day, we have always had our big gathering on New Year's Day. Grandma used to have the Christmas gatherings until she passed away in 1956. Then my mother had the New Year's Day meal, and now the tradition has been passed on to me. Grandma and Mother would both get up early New Year's morning to begin frying chicken for the hundred-plus people who would be in attendance. Grandmother and Grandfather had over a hundred grandchildren and great-grandchildren. My mother always said, "Serve them good, make sure there is enough food for everyone." And there was always plenty. This Church Windows recipe is one such holiday favorite to be enjoyed.

Church Windows for Christmas

Makes 2 dozen $3/4$-inch-thick slices

1/2 cup margarine or butter

1 (12-ounce) package chocolate chips

3 cups multicolored miniature marshmallows

1 cup chopped pecans

1 cup shredded coconut (optional)

In a double boiler over medium heat, melt the margarine and chocolate chips until creamy, stirring constantly (6 to 7 minutes). Remove from the heat and fold in the marshmallows. On a cookie sheet covered with a 24-inch-long piece of wax paper, spread the pecans and coconut evenly, leaving 2 inches of paper uncovered on each end and 1 inch uncovered on each side. Spread the chocolate mixture over the nuts and coconut. Let set for 5 minutes. Starting at one of the long ends, roll the paper gently toward the center, pulling the paper up as you roll, like a jelly roll. When you have rolled three-quarters of the way, bring the opposite side up and over the log. Refrigerate until firm, about 2 hours. Slice and serve.

Christmas in the Amish community isn't the materialistic affair that it is in most of the rest of the country. Walk into most Amish homes and you won't see a Christmas tree, lights, wreaths, or pine-scented garlands strung above the mantle. Adhering to their beliefs of following a simple sacrament, the Amish keep Christmas plain. In the Coblentz home, the only hint of the holidays are colorful Christmas cards sent by well-wishers that Elizabeth keeps on a shelf above her rocking chair in the living room.

When I was still living at home, Mother had a recipe for an older variation of a Long John Roll. She made what we call "lard cakes." Before we got the recipe for Long John Rolls, lard cakes were the favorite doughnut-type pastry around here. We fixed them on Butchering Day, when the pork is processed. We would put them in deep hot lard and fry them that way. But you have to eat them for breakfast, as they stale quickly. After dinner they weren't good to eat any more.

People don't use lard as much these days. The store-bought lard has more of a flat taste. I prefer fresh lard. When you butcher hogs, the lard has a good smell. Chunks of lard are cut off the hog, then cut into small pieces and put into a kettle to fry. If you then put the lard in a tightly sealed container, it will stay fresh for well over a year. I think lard tastes best in lots of things, especially pie crust (see page 127). Because Long John Rolls keep longer than lard cakes, they have become the favorite morning pastry around here.

I am not sure how Long John Rolls got their name, but they are good to eat on a cold winter's day when you might be wearing long johns. Leah is the one who first got the recipe for Long John Rolls, and she used to make them when she still lived at home and wasn't married. These sweet pastries are oblong in shape and when you are done making them, you frost them like a doughnut. You can make them any size.

Leah's Long John Rolls

Makes 3 dozen rolls

ROLLS

6 to 7 cups all-purpose flour

1/2 teaspoon salt

2 (1/4-ounce) packages active dry yeast

1 cup warm water

1 cup milk

1/2 cup margarine or butter

2/3 cup sugar

2 eggs, beaten

1/8 teaspoon ground nutmeg

FROSTING

2 tablespoons shortening

1 teaspoon vanilla extract

2 cups powdered sugar

To make the rolls, put 3 cups of the flour and the salt into a bowl, form a well in the center, and set aside. In a separate bowl, dissolve the yeast in the warm water. In a small saucepan over high heat, scald the milk until it gets a thin skin on top and then take it off the heat and let it stand to cool. In a mixing bowl, blend together the margarine, sugar, and eggs. Add the nutmeg. When the milk is lukewarm, add it to the sugar mixture. Then add the yeast and stir well. Pour this mixture into the well of flour and stir. Add 3 to 4 more cups of flour, 1/2 cup at a time, until the dough is easy to handle. Cover the dough with a loose piece of cheesecloth or plastic wrap and set in a warm, draft-free place to rise until double (about 90 minutes).

To make the frosting, combine the shortening, vanilla, and powdered sugar in a bowl and stir until smooth. Set aside.

To test the dough, lightly press two fingers $^1/_2$ inch into the dough. If the dent remains, the dough has doubled and is ready to use. Roll out the dough until it is $^1/_2$ inch thick. With a knife, cut oblong pieces about 3 or 4 inches long and 2 inches wide. Cover the pieces with a loose piece of cheesecloth or plastic wrap and set in a warm, draft-free place to rise again until double (about 40 minutes). Fry the pieces in a 6-quart kettle, preferably cast-iron, filled with oil or fat to the half or three-quarter mark. Fry up to three rolls at a time over medium heat until golden brown, about 2 to 3 minutes per side. Spread the frosting on the hot rolls and serve.

Corn-Husking Bee

Who knows what a corn-husking bee is? We used to go to these bees years ago. Some people still have them, but they aren't as common because fewer people are in farming nowadays.

At a corn-husking bee, the menfolk take a team of horses and a wagon to the cornfield when the harvest is ready to be husked. They jerk the ears of corn with the husk on and haul them back to the barn or a shed. They make a long pile of corn ready to be husked. In the evening, the young people are invited to help husk the corn by lantern light. Benches are set up in front of the corn, so the job can be done sitting down. The clean white husks go into a box to be kept clean. Then they are taken into the house to be put in a big sack with four openings in it. We stuff the husks inside the sack till it is full. These sacks are then used as a mattress by some.

There's lots of singing and yodeling all evening. After the corn is husked, everyone goes in the house for soup, sandwiches, and something to drink. There are still corn-husking bees today, but most people use regular store-bought mattresses. A few folks still have the husk-filled mattresses, but there's less dust with a store-bought one. It just depends on your preference.

The Amish Cook

by Elizabeth Coblentz

June 2000

This is a very beautiful, sunshiny Thursday morning, and I guess I should get this column in the mail today. Daughters Leah, Lovina, Emma, and their lovely children, came for the day today. Now the garden is getting a good weeding. What would I do without my family for support, especially as I write this letter with tear-stained eyes?

It's so hard to put this into words, but we must keep our faith in our Heavenly Father above. He will help us in such a time of our great loss, very great loss. It just doesn't seem this has taken place with my dear, beloved, calm, patient husband, Ben. Ben's gentle soul lives on in our broken hearts. Such a wonderful, supportive husband and father to all of us.

Lots of memories linger on, as we have to go on. Some readers, who lost spouses, told me in their letters to keep on going: don't sit and think. What would I do without the support of my two daughters, Verena and Susan, here at home? Verena takes over the chores, unless some of our married children are here. Our married children also have been so supportive.

Daughter Liz and her children spent the day here yesterday, and son Albert's family was here for supper yesterday. Joe's (daughter Lovina's) family came later in the evening and stayed for the night. So we're never alone, as it seems we're overnight someplace or someone in the family stays here overnight. How supportive!

I am so glad Ben didn't have to suffer long. God's ways aren't our ways. He's the One who never made or makes a mistake. He had a purpose to take Ben away from pain and, especially, worries, in this troublesome world we have to live in.

On Sunday, May 14, we got up early to start the day off. Ben did the morning chores as usual. And he then got the horse harnessed and hitched up to our new buggy, which he had purchased not too long ago, had breakfast, and then we went on to church services.

At lunch after services, Verena came and said, "Dad doesn't feel too good." So I got up and went to the table of men where he was seated. I asked, "Ben, aren't you feeling good?" And he just mumbled something and we saw right away there was something wrong. Our son Albert and son-in-law Paul got up from the table and carried Ben in a blanket into the yard. Someone else ran to a phone to call for help. Ben was admitted to a hospital, where they determined he had a stroke. But Ben's recovery was quick, and he was able to go home after an overnight stay. He came home and seemed alert.

He walked out to the barn on Wednesday morning and again on Thursday morning and was always worried to see that the cow got milked. He was always the one who, at 4:00 A.M., got out of bed to milk the cow. Such a nice week that God spared with us, that final week. Because on Saturday morning, May 20, I fed him two eggs, toast, two cups of homemade garden tea, and some applesauce. He seemed okay. But all at once, he began to breathe hard.

Emergency medical services were called again, but life had fled him before they came. So peaceful to see his eyes set on me and feel he was gone. Such a terrible feeling to lose a good husband. So many memories linger on. We had many good days together since we were married on October 17, 1957. Born to this union were eight lovable children: two sons, Amos and Albert; and six daughters, Mrs. Paul (Leah) Shelter, Mrs. Levi (Liz) Wengerd, Mrs. Joe (Lovina) Eicher, Mrs. Jacob (Emma) Schwartz, Jr., and Verena and Susan at home with me. How thankful to have them with me.

God has a purpose for it all. We must adjust to a different life. It sure has been different. Can't explain what it's like without my dear husband, Ben. Also, we have twenty-nine grandchildren. We had thirty, but dear little Mary left at five years old for a better home.

The funeral for Ben was on Tuesday, May 23, with around seven hundred people attending. Everyone was invited for dinner as usual. There were twelve tables set up for the dinner at noon in our tool shed. I feel we had so much good help from friends and relatives over this time for the loss of Ben. Thanks goes out to them who helped in our time of great loss.

I should thank all the readers out there for all the cards and gifts since the death of my dear husband, Ben. Words can't express the appreciation to you great readers out there.

On Sunday, this column's editor, Kevin Williams, and his mother brought over a thousand emails plus a thirty-two-gallon tub full of cards. The gifts will help with the hospital bills. Thank you all to be so supportive. I won't be able to write everyone to express my appreciation. But I hope this does it.

Good luck to all out there, 'til next time. We never know what the future holds. God only knows.

Beloved Ben

Ben's family moved to our area in the 1950s. We first met when we shared a buggy ride together with some other young folks. Ben worked on a dairy farm at one of our neighbors' places before doing a two-year stint (1953 to 1955) for war duty at St. Elizabeth Hospital in Lafayette, Indiana. The Amish are not exempt from the draft, but because of our pacifist religious beliefs, the menfolk are assigned to home-front duty in hospitals and factories during times of war.

After he was released from duty, Ben started in the carpenter trade. The work was slack after our marriage in 1957. I often think of 1958, when there were no earnings in January, February, and March. Life looked dull at times, but the Good Lord provided. Ben got more carpenter work later in the spring and ran a carpenter crew for many years doing new buildings and repair work of all kinds on barns, houses, sheds, garages, and you name it. There were long days of hard work, which he endured for over thirty years.

After he left carpentry, he worked on a dairy farm again for several years in the 1990s. During the last year of Ben's life, he retired, after having to battle a bout of pneumonia. It was good to have him at home as there was always repair work around the farm. At the age of sixty-nine it was time to retire some. He was a hard-working husband.

Note: We received over three thousand letters and five thousand emails from Elizabeth's newspaper column readers in the weeks following Ben's sudden death in May 2000. Elizabeth had often made mention of her husband and beloved partner during the ten years she's been writing her column. Readers felt they knew Ben; his gentle demeanor came through in Elizabeth's words. Following is "The Amish Cook" newspaper column that ran immediately after Ben's passing. I stepped in to write the column for Elizabeth that week to break the news to her readers.

The Amish Cook
by Elizabeth Coblentz

May 2000

Benjamin A. "Ben" Coblentz, 69, passed suddenly from this earth Saturday. Ben's wife, Elizabeth, who pens this weekly column, is still coping with the shock and grief.

I was nineteen years old in 1991, when I first pulled into Elizabeth's driveway one warm July afternoon. From that chance encounter, "The Amish Cook" column was born. I've been Elizabeth's editor ever since, and during that time, the Coblentzes have become practically family. I share in their weddings, births, and, sadly, deaths.

During my years of visiting the Coblentzes, I've been blessed to know Ben. Rare is the couple who remains affectionate and loving after forty-three years of marriage. But Ben and Elizabeth were that living rarity. Ben would affectionately tease Elizabeth (he called her "Lizzie") at the dinner table, and Elizabeth would give back as good as she got. Ben was Elizabeth's calm center. Elizabeth is the emotional one, but she was balanced by Ben's pragmatic peace. They were the perfect balance.

With a long white beard and weathered hands from decades of working as a carpenter, Ben was ever the supportive spouse. In a busy household of children and grandchildren, Ben would sit quietly in his rocker, with a soft smile and gentle demeanor, watching it all.

Ben and I were from two different worlds, yet I felt very close to him. I don't milk cows or cultivate the craft of carpentry as he did. I'm a city boy, more comfortable in my world of computers and cars. Yet we always found things to talk about. We could talk about baseball. We were both avid Cincinnati Reds baseball fans. I would visit with the latest news of trades or home runs and a smile would flicker across his face. He would show me his purple-martin houses or patiently let me follow him into the barn as he did the afternoon chores. It's hard to measure how much any one person impacts our lives. A life is a portrait comprised of brush strokes from the many people we pass. I look back at the

still incomplete portrait of my life, and some of what I am are the brush strokes of Ben. For that, I'll always be grateful.

Ben helped teach me to savor simplicity: the pleasure of a purple martin, the quiet calm of sitting on a rocker by a flickering fire, or scanning the starlit sky on a crisp, clear January night. In our increasingly material, twenty-first-century society, people measure their happiness by tangible things they can touch. For Ben, happiness could be found in the intangibles, in what he could not touch: a bird in flight, a grandchild's innocent heart.

Ben also was my secret ally. Editors often have trouble getting their writers to adhere to deadlines, and Elizabeth is no different from any other columnist. I like for Elizabeth to send her columns to me on Thursdays. If Thursday morning came, and the column had not been sent, Ben would be nudging Elizabeth out of bed early, envelope and stamp in hand, reminding her to write. Ben was very proud of Elizabeth's column.

The Coblentz farm is my retreat, a place I go to escape the noise of the sometimes rude world we live in. I stand on their porch and savor the pastoral peace of a landscape unbroken by power poles and listen to the rhythmic cadence of a passing horse's hooves. The peace seems to lend itself to infinity, an unchanging land, frozen in another century. If forever exists, it would be found on an Amish farm, where change is glacial.

Ben's gentle soul lives in his sons, Amos and Albert. If the legacy a loved one leaves is his or her children, then Ben can look down

from Heaven with happiness. All of his eight children are wonderful. In the baseball terms he loved, he's eight for eight. That's the best average one can ask for.

I was honored and deeply touched to be invited to the private cemetery ceremony where Ben A. Coblentz was laid to rest Tuesday, May 23, 2000. Driving to the ceremony, I turned on the emergency flashers and slowed to a crawl. A column of charcoal black horse-drawn buggies clattered on the road in front of me, moving slowly and solemnly. It was the surreal union of two worlds, as my car joined the funeral procession of buggies.

On any other day, I would be tapping my fingers impatiently on the dashboard, waiting for the slow-moving vehicle to get out of my way so I could speed to my destination. Instead, I was forced to take a deep breath and watch the peaceful, pristine Indiana countryside move by like a slow-motion movie. Century-old barns, gently burbling creeks and well-manicured meadows were a reminder there was once another time; a time when things were simpler, were quieter. But it's still there. We just never look.

Appendix: Basic Recipes

Salad Dressing

Makes 2¹/₂ cups

1 egg

1 tablespoon plus 1 cup water

²/₃ cup all-purpose flour

2 teaspoons dry mustard

²/₃ cup sugar

¹/₂ cup apple cider vinegar

³/₄ cup vegetable oil

1 tablespoon lemon juice

In a small bowl, lightly beat the egg with the 1 tablespoon of water. In a saucepan, mix together the flour, mustard, and sugar and toss with a fork to eliminate any lumps. Stir in the remaining 1 cup water and the vinegar, oil, and lemon juice. Heat over medium-high for 1 minute, stirring constantly. The dressing will be thick. Add the egg mixture and continue to cook for about 1 minute, stirring constantly, until the dressing has a mashed potato consistency and is off-white in color. Remove from the heat, cover with waxed paper, and cool completely. The salad dressing will keep for many weeks in a covered jar in the ice-house, or for those who have one, the refrigerator.

Homemade Mayonnaise

Makes 2¹/₂ cups

2 cups sugar

¹/₂ cup all-purpose flour

1 teaspoon salt

¹/₂ teaspoon ground mustard

1 cup water

4 eggs, beaten

1 cup apple cider vinegar

1 tablespoon butter

In a saucepan, blend together the sugar, flour, salt, and mustard over medium heat. Add the water and eggs and stir. Add the vinegar and stir. Add the butter and heat until the mixture boils. Boil until the mixture thickens. The mayonnaise will keep for many weeks in a covered jar in the ice-house or, for those who have one, the refrigerator.

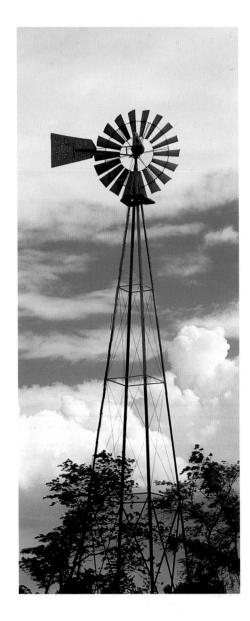

Cream of Mushroom Soup

Makes 4 cups

2 cups fresh mushrooms, chopped

1 small onion, chopped

2 cups chicken broth

3 tablespoons butter

3 tablespoons all-purpose flour

1 1/2 cups milk

1/2 cup cream

Salt

Pepper

In a large saucepan, combine the mushrooms, onion, and broth and heat over high heat for 1 minute. Decrease the heat to low and simmer, covered, for 15 minutes. Melt the butter in a small saucepan and stir in the flour to make a paste. Add the paste to the mushroom mixture and stir. Turn the heat up to medium and slowly add the milk, stirring constantly. When the mixture thickens and begins to boil, add the cream and stir. Cook gently until the mushrooms are tender. Season with salt and pepper to your taste.

Cream of Chicken Soup

Makes 5 cups

1/4 cup margarine or butter

5 tablespoons all-purpose flour

3 chicken bouillon cubes

3 cups boiling water

1/2 cup finely chopped cooked chicken

1 cup half-and-half

Salt

Pepper

Melt the margarine in a 1-quart saucepan over low heat. Blend in the flour. In a bowl, dissolve the bouillon cubes in the boiling water. Gradually add to the flour and margarine mixture. Stir until smooth. Add the chicken and bring to a boil over medium heat. Stir in the half-and-half. Season with salt and pepper to your taste.

Fresh Tomato Soup

Makes 2 quarts

2 cups sliced carrots

1 cup chopped celery

1 small onion, chopped

1/2 cup chopped green bell pepper

1/4 cup butter

4 1/2 cups chicken broth

4 medium tomatoes, peeled and chopped

4 teaspoons sugar

1/2 teaspoon curry powder (optional)

1/2 teaspoon salt (optional)

1/4 teaspoon black pepper

1/3 cup rice

In a large pot over high heat, sauté the carrots, celery, onion, and green pepper in the butter until tender. Add the broth, tomatoes, sugar, curry, salt, black pepper, and rice. Bring the mixture to a boil and then decrease the heat and simmer for 20 minutes.

Homemade Pizza Dough

Makes 1 pizza crust

2 cups all-purpose flour

2 teaspoons baking powder

1/2 teaspoon salt

2/3 cup milk

6 tablespoons vegetable oil

Preheat the oven to 425°. In a bowl, mix together the flour, baking powder, salt, milk, and oil. Stir vigorously until the mixture pulls away from the sides of the bowl. Gather the dough together and press into a ball. Knead the dough in the bowl 10 times until smooth. Flatten the dough evenly on a pizza pan or baking sheet, turning up and pinching or pleating the edge 1/2 inch all around. Add your favorite toppings and bake for 30 minutes, or until the toppings are done.

Mother's Pizza Sauce

Makes 10 cups

10 cups tomato juice

4 large bay leaves

1 large onion, diced

1/2 cup vegetable oil

1/4 teaspoon red pepper

1/2 teaspoon black pepper

4 tablespoons salt

2 teaspoons oregano

4 teaspoons sugar

1 1/2 teaspoons garlic powder

3/4 cup Clear Jel (see hint, page 131)

In a large saucepan, combine the tomato juice, bay leaves, and onion and cook over low heat for 20 minutes. Stir in the oil, peppers, salt, oregano, sugar, and garlic powder and bring to a boil over medium heat. Add the Clear Jel and stir. The sauce will change from a thin, runny consistency to a thicker, soupy consistency, and will be a pretty red. Return the sauce just to a boil over medium-high heat. As soon as the sauce begins to boil, remove it from the heat.

Quick Caramel Frosting

Makes 2 cups

4 tablespoons brown sugar

2 tablespoons butter

4 tablespoons milk

2 cups powdered sugar

In a saucepan, combine the brown sugar, butter, and milk and heat over low heat, until just boiling. Stir immediately and then remove from the heat. Let cool completely. Thicken the frosting with powdered sugar to your desired consistency.

Vanilla Frosting

Makes 3 cups

$1/2$ cup margarine or butter

1 egg

1 teaspoon vanilla extract

4 cups powdered sugar

3 to 4 tablespoons milk

In a bowl, beat together the margarine, egg, and vanilla until light and fluffy. Stir in the powdered sugar. Beat in the milk, 1 tablespoon at a time, until desired spreading consistency is reached.

About the Photographs

The photographs in this book were taken in or around the Indiana Amish community where Elizabeth and her family live. Unless otherwise noted, all photographs are by Laurie Smith.

Index

The Amish Cook

by Elizabeth Coblentz

May 2001

This leaves it a Sunday evening, May 20, 2001. It's a year ago now that my dear husband, Ben, was taken to that heavenly home. He's in a place where there's no more worry and pain, only peace. But I must go on.

Was glad to see daughter Emma and Jacob and family coming here last evening, Saturday, as it just made a better feeling to have someone come. They stayed for the night. So this morning we had breakfast together.

Didn't know if some other family members would show up for dinner, so we waited to start a dinner. Paul's (daughter Leah), Joe's (daughter Lovina) and Jacob's (daughter Emma) were our dinner guests. They had dinner here and stayed all day, leaving in the evening. It was a day well spent, together with family. Then to my surprise, Ben's sister and husband drove in and gave a visit.

Daughter Lovina will never forget her twenty-ninth birthday last year, May 22, as the funeral of Ben was the next day. So this was a quieter birthday this year.

Now the news of this evening: at 8:30 P.M. a daughter named Laura was born to son Amos and Nancy Jean, weighing 9 pounds, 8 ounces, and 22 and 1/4 inches in length.

She joins one brother, Ben, and seven sisters: Susan, Elizabeth, Mary Jane, twins Arlene and Marlene, Lovina, and Lisa. I suppose Amos's Ben would have been proud for a brother, but the baby is happy and healthy and that is all that matters. This makes thirty-three grandchildren living, one, Mary Shetler, deceased.

Now it looks a stormy Monday morning and the laundry was hung out on the clothesline early, only to bring the clothes back in because of the rain. I don't like to leave it hang when a storm comes up. It really rained and rained and then quit, so, again, the laundry was hung out and this time it all dried. Doesn't look like the rain is over with, though.

We are having plenty of rain lately. Had two inches of rain by noon.

Verena went over the property she owns to do some cleaning up and my youngest daughter, Susan, had been weeding flowers and wherever it needs it. Spring brings many tasks. What would we do without family?

A couple of readers recently have asked for recipes for apricot pie. Following is a good recipe:

Apricot Pie

Makes 1 (8-inch) pie

2 (8-inch) unbaked Never-Fail Pie Crusts
(see page 127)
2 cups dried apricots
2 cups water
1/2 cup sugar
1 1/2 tablespoons cornstarch
Pinch of salt
3 tablespoons butter

Preheat the oven to 425°. Roll out the crusts and use one to line an 8-inch pie pan, as directed on page 127. In a saucepan, bring the apricots and water to a boil over high heat. Cook for 10 minutes. Add the sugar and cook for another 5 minutes. Drain, reserving 1 cup of the juice. Set the apricots aside. Pour the 1 cup reserved apricot juice into a saucepan and add the cornstarch. Add the salt and cook over medium-high heat until the mixture thickens, stirring frequently. Arrange the drained apricots in the crust. Pour in the thickened apricot juice. Dot with the butter. Cover with the top crust and slit the top and flute the edges. Bake for 30 minutes, until the crust is golden brown on top.